OPERATION BREAKTHROUGH

How to Break Through Barriers and Position Yourself in Federal Government Contracting
How to Ease Your Transition into Federal Government Contracting
A Small Business Perspective!

OPERATION BREAKTHROUGH:

Striving through Struggles
for
SUCCESS
by
TEAMING

<u>COMMITMENT & SUCCESS</u>:

Proverbs 16:3—Commit to the Lord whatever you do,
and your plans will succeed
Isaiah 54 and Psalms 91

"Your dream will remain a mere image of what could be unless you
strive to achieve it."

Nathaniel "Nate" Couser, AWSIM
Army Veteran Captain

OPERATION BREAKTHROUGH

Striving through Struggles

for

SUCCESS

by

TEAMING

Nathaniel "Nate" Couser, AWSIM
Army Veteran Captain

authorHOUSE®

AuthorHouse™
1663 Liberty Drive
Bloomington, IN 47403
www.authorhouse.com
Phone: 1-800-839-8640

Published by AuthorHouse   06/17/2013

ISBN: 978-1-4817-6436-0 (sc)
ISBN: 978-1-4817-6437-7 (hc)
ISBN: 978-1-4817-6438-4 (e)

Library of Congress Control Number: 2013910843

Contents

PART I

THE DRIVE!

PART II

ENTREPRENEURSHIP!

PART III

THE TRADITIONAL WAY . . . MOST FAILURES OF SMALL BUSINESSES! THE PROCESS OF SMALL BUSINESS PENETRATION! UNDERSTANDING GOVERNMENT CONTRACTING, NOT FOLLOWING TRADITION TO FAILURE! BREAKING BARRIERS, OBSTACLES AND ADVERSITY!

PART IV

CONCEPT TO COMPLEXITY!
INNOVATION—TEAMING BY CREDIBILITY!

PART V

STRATEGIC BREAKTHROUGH!
PENETRATION / FORWARD INTELLIGENCE!

PART VI

STABILITY AND SUSTAINMENT TO SUCCESS! IMPACT—IMPORTANCE OF PROTECTION! SELF PROTECTION!

PART VII

INNOVATIVE RESOURCES!

TO: TAMMY
TO A FRIEND & BUSINESS
PARTNER THAT I WILL ALWAYS
KEEP CONNECTED WITH FOR LIFE!
I REALLY APPRECIATE YOUR SUPPORT!

THANKS,
NATE C.

DEDICATION

(To my Wife)

This book is dedicated to my Beautiful Wife who went through the struggles of the business world with me to achieve success. My Wife stood through the test of times; the everyday challenges a business can go through, surviving when there was a lack of funding to maintain our everyday living, contemplating whether we would make it through the struggles and adversities, wondering whether we would weather the business storm to maintain and sustain this business that I will describe throughout this book. I want to say that my Wife stood by me through all of this wondering whether we would make it through these challenging times that looked to have no end. When you reach a financial low, you find out who your friends really are as I always questioned various ones; it was like some friends presented a red flag—but you ignore it and discover who you can count on, as we found out. We have true friends that I will mention in this book that represent the ideal "True Friend".

During these times, regardless of the events that I am about to explain that occurred, I never swayed off track, never doubted for one minute because of my resolute faith that we would not reach our designation. My Wife stood by me every second, every minute, every hour, every day, every week, every month and every year by God's grace and we are still standing to our measure of success. This is a true commitment of fidelity and I appreciate my Wife's continuous support each and every day.

DEDICATION

(To my Children)

This book is to dedicate to my children for the moral support and structure that they represent. My children possess the finest qualities of role models to other children and adults. They are all productive and exceptional adults to any high standard of measures. They exceed the bar of any expectations to be classified as one of the best children to be raised into exceptional adults.

My children have illustrated an extraordinary strength of determination, faith, perseverance, persistence, endurance, tenacity and the agility to rise above any occasion towards their efforts of success in education and business.

I want to show my sincere gratitude to my children for providing me total support throughout this venture of the book and throughout my entrepreneurial pursuit of upward and downtimes towards my business success.

Stay in the fight of life and never give up your pursuit towards any dreams or ambitions you might believe in at your deepest times. Stay with your utmost faith and God will take you through any obstacles, struggles and adversity. Stay driven and focused for life!

DEDICATION

(To my Fellow Veterans & Soldiers)

Having previously served in the United States Army, Army National Guard, Army Reserves, and Joint Warfighter, I have remained dedicated to supporting active military and reservists of all branches; including service disabled veterans and veterans.

My company and I are mobilized and readily available to provide Entrepreneurship and total Career support to the masses. As serving in both ranks as an enlisted non-commissioned officer and as a commissioned officer I fully understand the forward intelligence of career and entrepreneurship for my fellow soldiers and veterans.

My company and I are dedicated to help as many Military Troops and Veterans as possible with their transition into the civilian environment. I have partnered with many organizations in order to bring you a total "one-stop shop" of resources and tools for Entrepreneurship.

This book will provide a tremendous amount of resources to help you transition into the challenging endeavor of Entrepreneurship!

I have stood and still stand beside you at all costs to support our country in our stand of freedom!

Take a further look to see the personal challenges I have endured, yet my willingness and perseverance to succeed. Hopefully, this will lend great inspiration to provide strength for you to succeed.

Let's move forward in this book to discover the journey that develops.

Preface

AN ENTREPRENEURIAL AND SMALL BUSINESS JOURNEY TO SUCCESS!

<u>Creative thinking and implementation in these nine (9) vital areas can get you to your entrepreneurial dreams:</u>

Determination

Failure

Faith

Perseverance

Persistence

Struggles

Success

Teaming

Tenacity

This book has been developed and designed to provide valuable resources, processes and methodologies to help Entrepreneurs and Small Business Owners to reach their levels of success in Public and Private Sector business. This book is developed to inspire and motivate the pursuit of entrepreneurship. It will illustrate how to position your business and minimize risk. You will learn how to establish your entrepreneurial path and embark on your journey to entrepreneurial success. You will understand how to overcome your fears, overcome adversities and challenges, break through business barriers, protection of your business and self, break bad habits to become victorious over self-defeating beliefs. In addition, you will learn to never to accept failure, and regardless of the obstacles faced, move up the success ladder. This methodology is an inspiration of entrepreneurial power within self, a motivated set of tools and resources, highly innovative and not the kind of success that normally gets handed down. Determination and hard work are the "keys"—it's a journey, not a destination.

The Author, having a multi-functional, diversified background of experience, was able to carve an entrepreneurial and small business niche of innovative sources of business solutions from one multi-functional collaborated system. In 2005, he launched his own firm by uniquely turning his struggles into success and implementing the methodology outlined in this book. In doing so, he hopes readers will gain valuable insight towards achieving their goals during these especially challenging times. Being that his entire military and civilian career placed him in unique positions that provided him great exposure to gain unlimited, unique and valuable business experiences from the best corporations in the world along with combined private, public and military. From being immersed in the trenches of learning success from being involved in the best in many different industries, the author has much insight to share. This is just one of the initial reasons why this book should be read by all entrepreneurs and small business owners.

This book describes the pathway through life's challenges, accomplishments, rewards, downfalls and successes to prevail through any obstacle that may come or continue to come our way.

This book describes how our life experiences developed through a path of challenges that initially derived from our decision of whether to sway from our dreams or to stay consistent to complete the journey.

This book describes the challenges we have faced to get where we are today and gave us the continuous drive to succeed even through the times that we should have given up. In this book, I will describe my real-life experiences as it relates to the challenges of developing a business through **"Operation Breakthrough: Striving through Struggles for SUCCESS by TEAMING™."** And believe me, there were many struggles that I will illustrate in this book. This book will explain that as long as you stay grounded in the Lord and have the undying love and support of a significant other, you can overcome anything and in fact, this is a testimony within its own context.

Initially, my situation seemed unique, yet isolated, yet common by unspoken experiences witnessed by others, but overall overwhelming in my efforts to strive for business success. My personal and business characters were of helping others first, then capturing my success by the support to others in a collaborative manner. My entire military and civilian careers have been in support of others. My entire military and civilian career has been in support of others. Naturally, in my career as an enlisted soldier to the advancement of a Commissioned Officer of the United States Army, my embedded values and experience increased by the responsibilities of protecting the interest of our country. My ability to gain business success extended from the loyalty of the ranks of self-driven motivation and trusting characteristics as accepting the oath to protect the country and serving as a measure of military protection.

My entrepreneurial journey created a tremendous amount of success. My success extended to a level of invaluable results. My methodologies, strategies and processes attracted the highest levels of business accomplishments that you can't purchase through monetary means. I guess what I am speaking of is not just contracts, even though that brought me to an unlimited reach in Government Contracting, but I am about talking about what other words can be classified as a success story? I am speaking of total collaboration in the form of the most innovative strategy, methodology or system process. This is what I have termed "OBT Strategic Teaming".

Let me provide you with some of the proven outcomes of this operational system:

- Developed a strong, strategic business foundation with supported and proven experts from multiple layers of success:
  o Advisory Board Members
  o Teaming Partners
  o Credible Business Relationships
- Achieved "Credibility by Teaming" without marketing, business development or branding
- Automatic Branding, Marketing, and Business Development
- Forecast Planning for Procurement opportunities without utilizing my own assets

- Developed a multi-functional and multi-layered structure of alignment of teaming partners, advisory board members, competitive intelligence sources in total alignment with my business service offerings

If this is not enough proof for you that these methodologies, systems and processes work like a fine, tuned engine, <u>then let me provide you with some more examples of proven success by recognition, confirmation and credibility:</u>

- A global services company that provides customers with access to products, insights and experiences that enrich lives and build business success having over 63,000 employees, world largest purchase volume company in the world, over $30 Billion in annual revenue and in over 130 plus countries and whose focus is to help small business owners to succeed.
- The oldest and largest national, nonprofit, non-partisan organization representing all Asian American and Asian American-related groups in business, sciences, the arts, sports, education, public and community services. They promote and propel economic growth to represent varied ethnic groups trace their heritage to United States, China, Hong Kong, Taiwan, Japan, the Philippines, South Korea, India, Indonesia, Vietnam, Cambodia, Thailand, Singapore, Malaysia, Bangladesh, Pakistan, and Mongolia.
- One of the world's largest Defense Contractor, 100 years of service; employs over 123,000 people worldwide. American global aerospace, defense, security, and advanced technology company with worldwide interests. They volunteered and became the major sponsor for my small business national workshop serving the purpose of helping

Entrepreneurs and Small Businesses to understand how to do business with the U.S. Government.

* With a focus on technology-based solutions, leader in aerospace and defense sector. Among its portfolios, it is responsible for training and simulation services for the U.S. military. Headquarters in the USA, and three other major offices in Australia, Asia and Europe, having over 93,000 professionals serving clients in more than 70 countries.

* The world's largest maker of equipment for building mobile telecommunications networks, with a market share of over 30%. It is one of Sweden's largest companies and provides telecommunications equipment, data communication systems, and related services covering a range of technologies including mobile networks.

* An employee base of 65,000 people working in more than 120 countries. The leading global provider of risk management, insurance and reinsurance brokerage, and human resources solutions and outsourcing services. The world's largest global insurance broker and No. 1 global reinsurance broker; global manager of captive insurance companies and global employee benefits consultant.

* More than 35 years of long-term growth with 71,000 professionals in 40 countries. Global delivery capabilities through centers located on 4 continents. Provide end-to-end IT and business process services that facilitate the ongoing evolution of our clients' businesses.

* Hundreds more of large companies, subcontractors, teaming partners, sponsors, and supporting companies and organizations that validated my overall Small Business Owners/Entrepreneur's solutions.

- The world's largest multi-channel consumer electronics retailer with stores in the United States, Canada, China, Europe and Mexico. The 10th largest online retailer in the U.S. and Canada having the number one customer loyalty program of its kind and more than 1.6 billion visitors their websites and stores each year. More than 165,000 employees committed to helping deliver the technology solutions that provide value, enabling access to people, knowledge, ideas and fun—whether online, via mobile device or in their stores.

By providing a source of mentorship to help other small business owners/entrepreneurs to be successful, this will allow you to develop at a much greater level of success. As I received greater success, soon after came the challenges of business and the trying of my faith to withstand the adversity that followed. You have to always remember that the "Measure of Success" is not how you receive a challenge; it is how you respond to the challenge. Remember that any business dimension will change by its environment so remaining flexible and agile to your surroundings and adapting to overcoming barriers is required in order to reach your level of success.

Remember, it's not just about how many contracts you accumulate, or how much your contracts are valued; it is what you have built to provide you the diverse and dynamic ways to your path to success. Don't let anyone deter your path, stay focused and continue to your road to success.

COMMITMENT & SUCCESS:

Isaiah 54:17 and Proverbs 16:3
*"Your dream will remain a mere image of what could be
unless you strive to achieve it."*
-Nathaniel "Nate" Couser, AWSIM
Veteran Army Captain

Acknowledgments

First of all, I want to gratefully acknowledge the presence of God for allowing me to address the continuous challenges, dealing with horrendous situations and being victorious in overcoming adversity to develop such a useful book that will enhance the business abilities for the many Entrepreneurs, Small Business Owners and any persons seeking to venture into entrepreneurship.

I would like to thank my wife, Stephanie, for her steadfast strength of faith, inspiration and consistent support to continuously pray for the clarity of such unexpected adversity. Special thanks to my sons, Natario (Dr. Couser), his Wife (My Daughter-in-Law)—Deanna (Dr. Couser) and Taurice, and my daughters, Crystal and Fallyn for their support, inspiration and prayers. Special acknowledgement to my daughter Crystal for overcoming such a tragedy by the grace of God to illustrate such perseverance to reach her ambitions. A special thanks to my mother (Evelyn) and stepfather (Eric) for their support. A special thanks to my brother, SFC Ronnie Couser, USA.

A special thanks to and support from family members such as my niece, Tasha Dennis, my niece, Terri Seals and nephew Robert Seals, SSgt. (Ret.) USA and nephew, Garrett Dennis.

A special, sincere gratefulness for the contributions of many who have gone before, those who constructed the knowledge and will of tenacity to make this book and its content possible to come forth.

A special thanks to my Pastor Ricky Texada for his relentless prayers and support at all times of overcoming adversity, pre and post success and special thanks to Senior Pastor Mike Hayes. Also special thanks for my friend of 30 plus years, Robert Sessom; and other important professionals as follows: Don Carter, Danny Portee, Danny Lovelady, LTC. (Ret.), Dennis Greene COL (Ret.) USAF, Brigadier General Wayne Wright USAF/VANG—Chief of Staff, LTC. Robert Campbell, PhD USAF, Ronald Graves COL. (Ret.) USAF, Dr. Marilyn Gowing, David Morris, Judge (Ret.) Roger McMillin, Monica Coney, Howard Ady COL (Ret.) USAR, Sam Evans COL (Ret.) USAF, Mershelle Davis, Jim Tanksley, Jenny Vallner, James T. George COL (Ret.) USAR, Norris Middleton Lt. COL (Ret.) USAR, Randy Smith, Frank Voigt, Christopher Faye, Aaron Morrison, Joan Turrisi, Randy Lange, Clifford Link, Dan Sturdivant (Ret.) USMC, Roger Skrobeck, Mark Envani, Kris Lonborg, Attorney Milton Colegrove, Attorney Ryan Cole, Attorney John Browning, Mark Szanca, Dr. Roger Channing, Matt Garcia, Julie Novak, William Gauntt, John Woosley, Jonathan Greene, Milli Brown, my Covenant Church Life Team Group, General Manager of Best Buy—Ken Macomber and Staff, and the Distinguish Gentlemen—Tuskegee Airmen and Chapter President COL. Calvin Spann and Attorney Ray Jackson and Staff and others.

A special thanks to my fellow veterans and soldiers for accepting the ultimate challenges to ensure freedom for our country adjusting to take on greater challenges of transitioning to the world of entrepreneurship.

Although there is not enough room to list all of you individually, I would like to thank the many True Friends, Teaming Partners, Advisory Board Members, Entrepreneurs, Small Business Owners, Organizations and Universities who have supported me throughout.

The Entrepreneur's Creed

We, as Entrepreneurs, seek to conquer our quest of success through the strength of our defined business intelligence. Make certain you develop an overall sense of business structure that will fit in today's environment, but will advance tomorrow's future in order to add an intellectual source that can endure for decades to come. We, as Entrepreneurs, seek to achieve the impossible to gain what no other has or can accomplish. To reach our goals is just merely a step towards success. Take each step with a sense of urgency but with a reality of precision driven by knowledge captured. Our operation carries a sense of total collaboration of many to achieve the mission for all!

We, as Entrepreneurs, peer through a vision that others can't visualize to achieve success. Have a sense of imagination to achieve the unlimited resources of success. Without imagination there will be a lack of creation—think massive and capture at a substantial level. We, as Entrepreneurs, through our pursuit of success always have to fully understand that in order to achieve the ultimate levels of success, we have to engage our strongest abilities, knowledge, innovativeness and tenacity towards accomplishing due diligence, or "homework."

We, as Entrepreneurs, are the driving force of our economy; the innovative, forward, transformative thinking for today and tomorrow. We are the pathfinders for the future and part of the generation that makes our country the most powerful on Earth.

We, as Entrepreneurs, must let everyone hear our roar without making a sound, let everyone see our visionary success without announcing but use our sheer presence. By the merit of our achievements, we are a force that drives without a pushing mechanism. We are a force that can't be reckoned with when we have total alignment. In other words, we are the future catalyst that creates the innovativeness for our future going forward with a source of intelligence that we call **"Operation Breakthrough."**

Introduction

Small Business Owners/Entrepreneurs traditionally start their businesses highly motivated, extremely excited, eager to launch into the business world and ready to reach the peak of success. Initially, they possess a tremendous amount of determination and tenacity to overcome any struggles that may come onto their path. They possess a great drive of persistency to visualize the achievement levels towards their success no matter what adversity appears in their lives. They attempt to think in a multi-functional framework towards all obstacles that they logically can think of at the launch of their entrepreneurial journey. They possess a high level of extreme tunnel vision of success and do not want to invite failure into their mindset and frame of planning. While slightly nervous, but overly anxious and vigorous, they take the leap of faith to explore the world of entrepreneurship and innovativeness. They have a great inspiration to become one of the most unique, exemplary individuals to receive the classified with acknowledgement that they have to earn the classification, with meaning behind it, to retain and sustain full entry into the mass group of professionals known as "Small Business Owners" or "Entrepreneurs". After all of the excitement to achieve an initial status of business success to unlimited growth, to strategically generate a driven process to stand on the pedestal of directional accomplishments of business, all to reach the apex of success seems to be just a time of forwardness.

Based on the struggles, obstacles, adversities, limitations, difficulties and misfortunes that will come your way in the big scheme of things, I am here to let you know by experience and reality of the harsh business world that these destructive situations will arise in a small package form or by the means of unknown manners or by people you do not expect to oppose your process of success through greed, reality of incredulity and the incertitude of loyalty of the unexpected individuals closest to you in business. There are limited positive, influential individuals readily available to support your entrepreneurial journey and a much greater pool of negative, cutthroat, polished, professional business people. Listen to my entrepreneurship story of reality, my means to accomplish success and my proven ability to achieve success over the struggles of business and life. After reading my book, adopt a strategic and innovative means to overcome all struggles of business by developing a "Teaming" methodology that will produce unlimited resources and solutions. Extensively execute your due diligence and research to eliminate and prevent the outcome of failure. Continuously gain and redefine knowledge about your business from an internal standpoint and all aligned external intelligence.

Most importantly, create an innovative business Foundation, Structure, Support Structure, Collaborated Resource Model and a Multi-Functional Strategic Operational Process. Maximize the benefits of Strategic Teaming and your struggles will be minimized. Save your time, money and efforts by avoiding repeated failed processes, lack of pursuit to business knowledge and incorrect services to invest in proven methods of success. Read on to explore the perfect solutions to your everyday business challenges.

PART I

<u>THE DRIVE!</u>

Chapter 1

Setting the Tone

Discuss the efforts and dedication it will take to start your business.

As a Small Business Owner/Entrepreneur, it is difficult for you to not meet expectations to reach your desired level of success and greater impact to your business when you get slammed by obstacles, adversities and struggles. You have to remain steadfast to your understanding of tenacity that failure is not in your business system of operation. You learn from it when it appears, and only acknowledge failure as a temporary state of condition.

<u>The Efforts required to start your business:</u>

Your efforts should be adopted with principles of unlimited drive, motivation and patience. You should define a set of rules of self-persuasion to accomplish any task that is needed to generate a successful, initial launch of your business as follows:

- You will hear this constantly: "Do your Homework!"
- Consistently and thoroughly perform your required "Due Diligence."

- Build all of your support structures for your business with strength of knowledge, but with the flexibility to be agile.
- Break all business barriers; do not go around them or the barriers will crush both your business and your dreams.
- When you come up against a wall of problems, which you will, don't let them stand in your way. Construct a breakthrough and log all information, so if you come up against the same problem again, you have the solution for future reference.
- Don't let anyone deter or discourage you from your mission to start your business.

The dedication required to start your business:

Most people know prior to starting their business that it is a big step, but Small Business Owners/Entrepreneurs understand that this is a huge undertaking and they initially execute partially correct. What they lack is full dedication to support their business adventure. This is mostly because they have yet to truly define what it really takes to develop a business prior to fully engaging total dedication for their business. Business is a full-time commitment and it should be understood that it may take excess of 60 to 70 hours a week and even weekends of your time to accomplish the initial launch of your business. However, it does get better once you start the business. Your hours will increase and the demands will increase to 24 hours a day, 7 days a week. You have to be able to manage your sleep hours more than work hours because the work hours will dominate your time.

Here are a few tips to help you stay dedicated while starting your business:

- No matter how pressing the demands from your business may become, stay balanced with your family.
- Remember if you have a bad day related to business, God willing, you will have another day to strive for excellence
- Your goals and ambitions are within your abilities to perform; don't let anyone have the power over you to keep them buried in you.
- Personal Responsibility: Small Business Owners/ Entrepreneurs, you can fail many times, but it takes the one time to get up again to achieve success!

Discuss the commitment it will take to endure the journey.

The commitment needed to endure through your entrepreneurial journey will require more patience and a host of other obligations that you probably hadn't even thought of for your business to prevail. There will be many a long night of working on the concepts, ideas and tasking to achieve, a lot of times, just basic tasking for your business. The particular mentioning of "obligations" extends throughout your entire business lifecycle. So don't expect that they will stop once you reach a certain level of your business, they will actually increase. Each business will require some of the same obligations, but depending on your business specialty, it may require a particular type of obligation.

<u>Here are several obligations to think about during your entrepreneurial journey:</u>

- While conducting your business, remember that you will always remain responsible for the financial obligations of the business.
- You must accept all responsibilities, including legal responsibilities that may impact your ability to conduct business.
- You have to set the limitations of information as to what to retain or what to release to others.
- You have to maintain the highest tolerance of patience in order to deal with the opposition you will encounter during your journey.
- You must be motivated more than anybody about your business.
- You must be 100% engaged in your business to ensure your success.

We cultivate, implement, exercise and execute our practice of future entrepreneurship as we go through the process of running our households and raising our kids. If we do not give up then, why would we give up in business? We raise our kids until they become 18 years of age and some until 21. Then, there are some we raise until an even older age due to continuation of school or merely to coach and nurture them since it takes longer until they reach a state of independence. This is the same basis that can be applied to a business process. There is a certain level of completion that your business must reach. The same standards you hold for how you raise your children, you must apply them to your business without the slightest notion of accepting failure, and your business should connect to your lifeline as well as conceptually be the end result.

- The tearing down of an Entrepreneur brings power to his tactics.
- When you lose control, you lose your ability to create.

To succeed in business, you have to be committed to putting in the hard work and due diligence necessary to build a business from the foundation up. You have to commit to your beliefs, faith and desires. You have to commit to your business strategies and ideas and you have to commit to your company's staff. Remember that you not only affect your family, staff and other supporting businesses, but their families as well. This commitment is a serious undertaking. With commitment comes effort and the ability to empower, with effort comes the tenacity to reach your results, and with results comes the power of success!

The Drive and Motivation of an Entrepreneur

Most entrepreneurs are overly optimistic about their reach for success, but those who try to reach a high level of growth are more likely to accomplish their reach for success than those do not even attempt to try. The drive and motivation of an entrepreneur normally comes with a high ability of risk-taking. A great example of a motivated entrepreneur would be when he or she takes a risk and starts a business even in economically challenging times. The idea of this matter is that if he or she never started the business, then they would never win because they never would have taken the risk. Highly motivated and self-driven entrepreneurs are most of the time recognized by their character. They are often very ambitious in their conversations when speaking of reaching various goals, but at the same time, the best entrepreneurs are very logical in their risk taking venture. They are always calculating their risk, but always overly innovative and persistent to win if not the first time, they will try again the second time and many more until they reach success. A great entrepreneur learns each time they miss the mark. The striking point here is that optimism is often a self-satisfying prediction in a world where an elite uniqueness of people are willing to take such tremendous risks, and those entrepreneurs who reach out for those self-seeking goals tend to do better than their counterparts.

By the sheer experience of being around a lot of entrepreneurs, I took notice that the best entrepreneurs were very successful because their motivation to be successful was attracted to the types of business that were extremely interesting, stimulating, exciting, challenging or provided a sense of total engagement on a high personal level. From my experience and interaction with other successful entrepreneurs, I realized that they all had the similar motivation of business obsession, fixation and a high level of enthusiasm to achieve success. This is normally the reverse for people who are extrinsically motivated, driven by expected evaluation, supervision, competition, awards or rewards. Entrepreneurs do what they do because they genuinely enjoy it and like to win no matter the opposition. They are internally competitive by nature.

A lot of entrepreneurs feel that it is their social responsibility to make a difference in their particular community, city, state, national or globally. They want to leave a legacy, but with the merit of them achieving such a great level of success by self-driven motivation and an internal nature of strong values. As mentioned above, those willing to risk both time and financial resources do so because they believe in what they're doing no matter what others may say to or about them. And with entrepreneurs like the late Steve Jobs, they have a desire to leave the world a better place by contributing innovations that improve the entrepreneur's chosen industry, a great will to help others and the ability to take the greatest risk. These individuals, who may possess nearly extreme levels of ambition, tend to provide products and services that strive to improve society and in the process leave a significant mark on the world. In short, they want to leave a legacy for tomorrow's future. This is my total concept of entrepreneurial thinking and what my business logic (OBT Strategic Teaming™) is partially built on for success.

<u>From the characteristics to the attributes of their values that I feel that successful entrepreneurs have in common:</u>

- **Dealing and Accepting of Constructive Criticism and Rejection**

  Innovative entrepreneurs are most of the time at the forefront of their prospective industries and mostly they always hear sorts of criticism: "it can't be done," "you do not have what it takes," "it will not work," "that is not a great idea," and various other statements that go into one ear and out the other. You listen to it, but you do not hear it or rotate it into your scheme of things. If it is worthy of substance, then a great entrepreneur will engage it into the alignment of the business. But they will verify and validate and verify again for certainty. They will take the criticism to evaluate for constructive value and determine whether it's useful to their overall plan. Otherwise, they will simply disregard the comments and keep moving forward towards success. Also, the best entrepreneurs know that rejection, adversity, struggles and obstacles are a part of the entrepreneurial journey and they deal with them appropriately.

● **Highly Self-Motivated and Energetic**
Entrepreneurs are always on the move, full of energy, self-driven, forwardly focused and highly motivated. They are driven to succeed and have an abundance of self-determination. Their standards are extremely high, yet they continuously aim higher then needed since their ambition demands excellence.

● **Internal Drive**
Entrepreneurs are driven to succeed and have a tremendous amount of internal motivation and a willingness to strive above any opposition. They see the bigger picture clearly, the direction they are headed and are often very ambitious. Entrepreneurs set massive strategic goals for themselves and stay committed to achieving them regardless of the obstacles that get in the way. They are normally multi-thinkers.

● **Strong Inner Beliefs and Relentless Faith**
Successful entrepreneurs have a healthy opinion of themselves and often have a strong and assertive personality. However, a lot of times, they seem to be

reserved, and prefer to take on a more observing approach. They are focused and determined to achieve their goals and believe completely in their ability to achieve them. They have an absolutely strong measure of faith. They believe internally that nothing can obstruct their path to success.

* **Innovation**

Most entrepreneurs have a passionate desire to do things better creatively and to improve their products or service through the highest level of innovation. They are constantly looking for ways to improve their ideas, concepts, methods, processes, systems and overall business. They're creative, innovative, resourceful, and will find a way to make things better no matter what stands in their way.

* **Flexibility**

When things are not working properly for them, entrepreneurs simply adjust, realign or adapt to the new change. Entrepreneurs know the importance of keeping on top of their industry and the key to being number one is to evolve and adjust with the changing times. They're up to date with the latest technology and are always ready to change if they see a new opportunity arise. They are also extremely focused on the mission of success.

* **Competitive by Nature**

Successful entrepreneurs thrive on challenges and competition. Most work better when the pressure is higher. They seek out the challenges and do not wait for them to come to their door. They measure all odds, analyze the different simulated wins and pick out the best choice for the occasion. They see no way of losing, but if their measurement of success falls short, then they recalculate and adjust for success.

One of the main reasons that the most successful entrepreneurs can build incredibly successful companies is that they really measure all that they have and calculate it so they don't have anything to lose by replacing it with higher outcomes of business success. The entrepreneur usually has a mortgage, car payment or a particular lifestyle to maintain, but they measure the success outcome to be much greater than what they possess to achieve a total mindset of greater possessions and the higher ability to help many others.

On the contrary, some entrepreneurs that are starting a company later in life have everything to lose. By this time in their career, they are used to a steady salary. They live in a nice neighborhood with a comfortable or even luxury car with a monthly payment attached, maybe kids in college, many investments, but they have the desire to take an intelligent risk for their business. When his/her spouse thinks about starting a new company, he/she will also consider the stark reality of losing the comforts of life that they have worked hard to build up during their career. Suddenly, when thinking about all that he/she has to lose, the experienced entrepreneur's plan to build a successful company include calculated moves, still a high-level risk, but vetted risk and a willingness to check all aspects of business failure, so as to not only get caught up in the success. If they rule out the majority of failures, then the only thing left is "success." There is a lot of unknowns to be defined.

When they have calculated there is nothing to lose, the entrepreneur can look at solving problems with a completely different mindset.

There is very little at risk because they validate all paths of success and failure. And only the thing that crosses the entrepreneur's mind is the drive to solve the identified problem in the best way possible. Fortunately, the entrepreneur has the energy to consistently burn the midnight oil by the unbound limits of their motivation and drive to success.

Analyze and evaluate your journey by unofficially discussing it with others to receive feedback about your journey.

There are many ways to validate your entrepreneurial journey to ensure the ability to reach your goals pertaining to your business. It can be direct or indirect and official or unofficial. My opinion is to use all four measures of evaluation. When planning, implementing and executing anything in reference of your business, always implement at a minimum three systems forms of checks and balances such as a "check, validate and verify" type system. Typically, whether in a direct or indirect means of a business evaluation, you will find out that your results will directly be given in a professional and technical manner. Always review the results, but you can almost guarantee every time that you can validate it with facts.

When an individual or a group or organization conducts an evaluation in an indirect manner, you will find out multitudes of great feedback, opinions, suggestions, criticism and sometimes proven experiences and accomplishments. Now you will also get a lot of false and inaccurate information. Again, validate and verify!

Often and frequently, you will receive a lot of unofficial feedback about your entrepreneurial journey whether you ask for it or not. This is good because you do not have to state your opinion on what you think. Just receive, observe and analyze for constructive feedback or criticism.

A great way to evaluate the credibility of preliminary feedback and detailed evaluations is to discuss your entrepreneurial journey with reliable and trusted sources.

Some of your greatest sources should be as follows:

- Other successful Entrepreneurs
- Other successful Business Owners
- Your Advisory Board
- Your Board of Directors
- Your Trusted Business Oriented Family Members and Friends

Always stay professional in appearance during any type of evaluation or receiving someone's opinion about your entrepreneurial journey. Always maintain a high level of professionalism while conducting your business or even in a personal environment related to business. A lot of times, you can gauge the character or value of others by the nature of their actions in a personal or business environment. Once you get personable while in a business environment or your personal persona becomes unprofessional in any shape or form, you allow yourself to be put in a comprising situation. This allows a great measure of feedback to scrutiny and issues related to negative drama that is bound to set in.

Bring all to agreement that will be involved in the business journey.

From the beginning brainchild of simply forming the thoughts to start a business, having the ability to turn your ideas into strategies, methodologies and processes to launch the initial phases of your business and throughout the entire process of your business cycle, absolutely always make certain of total agreement between all involved business members. You may have different opinions or means to get something accomplished for the business among all members involved, but never leave a single phase of decision making or "decision to execution", or "decision to proceed" to move forward to the next phase without total buy-in or total agreement.

When accomplishing a total agreement among all business members of your organization, you should consider the following tips:

- Empower by encouraging voting to receive the majority opinion, but also discuss any opposing opinions prior to going forward, so that hopefully everyone at least understands the decision to go forward and supports that decision.
- You can empower certain Advisory Board Members individually to make minor decisions.
- Make sure all agreements that require a lawful decision among business members are legally signed and witnessed or notarized. Make certain the agreements are created by an attorney.

- Schedule frequent meetings to make certain everyone understands and maintain an agreed upon direction of the business.
- Send out periodic surveys to all business members of your organization to get a majority opinion on upcoming decisions.

To maintain a successful flow of your business processes, you should make certain that members of your business are all of the same type of values, beliefs and ideas. Their priorities should be to always come to an agreement in a timely manner to keep the business flowing forward.

PART II

<u>ENTREPRENEURSHIP!</u>

Chapter 2

The Journey for the Entrepreneur

What is Entrepreneurship?

Definition: The act of being an entrepreneur can be defined as "one who undertakes innovations, finance and business acumen in an effort to transform innovations into economic goods."

Entrepreneurship is more than simply "starting a business." The definition of entrepreneurship is a process through which individuals identify opportunities, allocate resources and create value. This creation of value is often through the identification of unmet needs or through the identification of opportunities for change.

Entrepreneurs see "problems" as "opportunities," then take action to identify the solutions to those problems and the customers who will pay to have those problems solved. This takes a unique and innovative strategic way of thinking.

Entrepreneurial success is simply a function of the ability of an entrepreneur to see these opportunities in the marketplace, initiate change (or take advantage of change) and create value through solutions. This is defined as the assumption of risk and responsibility in designing and implementing a business strategy or starting a business.

Entrepreneurship vs. Small Business

Many people use the terms "entrepreneur" and "small business owner" synonymously. While they may have much in common, there are significant differences between the entrepreneurial venture and the small business.

Entrepreneurial ventures differ from small businesses in the following ways:

1. Amount of wealth creation—rather than simply generating an income stream that replaces traditional employment, a successful entrepreneurial venture creates substantial wealth, typical in excess of several million dollars of profit, sometimes billions.
2. Speed of wealth creation—while a successful small business can generate several million dollars of profit over a lifetime, entrepreneurial wealth creation often is rapid; for example, within 5 years.
3. Risk—the risk of an entrepreneurial venture must be high; otherwise, with the incentive of sure profits, many entrepreneurs would be pursuing the idea and the opportunity that no longer would exist.
4. Innovation—entrepreneurship often involves substantial innovation beyond what a small business might exhibit. This innovation provides the venture the competitive

advantage that results in wealth creation. The innovation may be in the product or service itself, or in the business processes used to deliver it.

In an extreme state, an entrepreneur is a person of very high aptitude who pioneers change, possessing characteristics found in only a very small fraction of the population. Other extreme definitions of an entrepreneur include anyone who wants to work for himself or herself.

My knowledge and experience as an entrepreneur provides me with clear understanding that an entrepreneur is born and has the internal traits to develop as an entrepreneur. But based on their journey of life, this rare astonishment can either be driven away from the person or it can be enhanced. You see, a true entrepreneur will find a way through any adversity to succeed in their quest for entrepreneurship.

As an entrepreneur, if you believe, God gives each of us entrepreneurs a source of discernment to understand signs/ warnings. I definitely know this because in my journey of entrepreneurship, every step of the way, through good and bad times, my strong faith has taken me and others to the levels of success that is truly unbelievable by normal, human standards. A word to the wise is to truly stay constant and steadfast to your belief of success no matter what discouragement you receive in your path. The greater the success, the more adversity will come your way to tear you down, stall your success or even take you completely off your success journey.

As an "Entrepreneur," you should be very knowledgeable of many areas of your business in both an inner layer and outer layer of business. The art of success in entrepreneurship is to make sure you retain as much knowledge as possible in all areas that surround your business and then overlap and align your business with professionals in all layers of your business. There are several, creative ways to bring these tremendous added-value propositions into your business without cost, which I will be discussing these techniques later in the book. As you build your series of strategic alignments, always make certain they come from the three areas of business: Core, Inner and Outer Layers.

Some areas of concentrated attributes:

- Advisory
- Customer service
- Finance
- Innovativeness
- Law
- Leadership
- Market positioning
- Quality
- Relationship building
- Resource building
- Teaming logic
- Unique concept building

Responsibilities of an Entrepreneur

There are so many responsibilities of an Entrepreneur that most people do not fully understand. There is a lot of information among the Internet and myriad books to explain many areas of entrepreneurship, but experiencing a real-life situation of duty is completely different. As you experience the highs and lows of the position, you will see the increase in uniqueness of responsibilities that is not freely advertised in the wide spread marketplace that comes to fruition in reality.

Without burdening you with the many unannounced responsibilities, I will provide a few examples as follows:

- You are the protector of your business and whatever happens in and around your company is solely your responsibility (good or bad.) No matter what business entity you choose, you will ultimately be carrying the burden of responsibility.
  - Large companies: You wonder why large companies have a host of attorneys and staff handling known and unknown issues.
  - Small Businesses: Most can't afford an Attorney, especially a staff of Attorneys, but small businesses want to pursue large contracts. When this happens, you need to have that legal support and most Small Businesses still have to utilize Attorney services. If not executed correctly, the proper security of the law is not secured while conducting business. This can be a major problem. Example: Small Businesses encounter many unexpected situations that can take them out of business in a day. Solution: Partner with a Law Firm so that they understand you and your company. By utilizing this method, they will be able to most likely support you at

a lower cost because they will already be familiar with you and your company.

- Normally, "CEO/Small Business Owner Protection" is the least talked about. This is extremely crucial in your entrepreneurial venture. We all seek to conduct business with the utmost consideration of integrity, honesty and loyalty. However, don't assume that you have total support from a business partner or partners. Assume the best, but prepare for the worst and unexpected situation.

- Frequently, if not in just about all cases, small business owners/entrepreneurs do not place the proper limitations and protection between one or more business partners.

- The majority of entrepreneurs take for granted that family and friends will be their best advocates for support. If somehow you find yourself in a legal battle, even when you are not at fault or find yourself in a less than optimal financial situation related to your business, you will see the total outcome of whether that family member or friend is truly on your side. As I refer to in the book as, "True Friends," they will support you to the end. Again, I am speaking as to when you are truly not at fault. A supportive person will get all of the necessary facts, speak directly to you about the situation prior to just assuming the negative information they hear about you directly or indirectly.

An Entrepreneurial Journey to Success

Creative thinking and implementation in the following nine, vital areas can get you to your entrepreneurial dreams:

- Determination
- Failure
- Faith
- Perseverance
- Persistence
- Struggles
- Success
- Teaming
- Tenacity

This book is designed to inspire and motivate the pursuit of entrepreneurship. It will illustrate how to position yourself and minimize risk. You will learn how to establish your career path and embark on your journey to entrepreneurial success. You will understand how to overcome your fears, break bad habits and be victorious over self-defeating beliefs. In addition, you will learn never to accept failure, and regardless of the obstacles faced, move up the success ladder. This methodology is an inspiration and not the kind of success that just gets handed to you in life. Determination and hard work are the keys—it's a journey, not a destination.

Entrepreneurship:

My personal Definition of an "Entrepreneur" is based on experience and ability to be in the trenches with other Entrepreneurs both in success and failure:

An Entrepreneur is someone that:

- o Develops an entire business with or without the proper resources, while locating and defining the scope of business progress to success;
- o develops the entire structure of the business;
- o can adapt to change and flexibility as the business environment shifts;
- o not only has the vision to see the current environment of political affairs, but also is able to forecast the direction in which the political landscape may impact their business;
- o gathers the correct tools and resources to manage the business;
- o if not properly educated for their business, will get the education that is needed to be successful;
- o will have to remain accountable and responsible for every aspect of their business;
- o will help others in their business venture and will take care of their staff to maximum security;
- o will take the negative, and there will be negatives, in stride and still motivate others even in the darkest hours, days, months or years.
- o If you don't know what it takes to be an entrepreneur, then you will never be able to define the true meaning of an "entrepreneur."

My definition is more defined because the contents and reality of pursuing "Entrepreneurship" is greater in definition because the focal point of the central word defines the impact of one's ability to fulfill this role of responsibility. Below, you will find the traditional definitions from historical organizations over time.

Historical Definitions of "Entrepreneur" or "Entrepreneurship"

Merriam-Webster Definition: one who organizes, manages and assumes the risks of a business or enterprise.

Web Definition: Entrepreneur is someone who organizes a business venture and assumes the risk for it.

Wikipedia Definition: Entrepreneurship is the act of being an entrepreneur or "one who undertakes innovations, finance and business acumen in an effort to transform innovations into economic goods." This may result in new organizations or may be part of revitalizing mature organizations in response to a perceived opportunity. The most obvious form of entrepreneurship is that of starting new businesses (referred to as Start-up Company); however, in recent years, the term has been extended to include social and political forms of entrepreneurial activity. When entrepreneurship is describing activities within a firm or large organization it is referred to as intra-preneurship and may include corporate venturing, when large entities spin-off organizations.

Characteristics of Entrepreneurs have many of the same character traits as leaders, similar to the early, great man theories of leadership; however, trait-based theories of entrepreneurship are increasingly being called into question. Entrepreneurs are often contrasted with managers and administrators who are said to be more methodical and less prone to risk-taking. Such person-centric models of entrepreneurship have shown to be of questionable validity, notwithstanding as many real-life entrepreneurs operate in teams rather than as single individuals. Still, a vast amount of literature studying the entrepreneurial personality found that certain traits seem to be associated with entrepreneurs:

- **Bird**—mercurial, that is prone to insights, brainstorms, deceptions, ingeniousness and resourcefulness. They are cunning, opportunistic, creative and unsentimental.
- **Busenitz and Barney**—prone to overconfidence and over generalizations.
- **Cole**—found there are four types of entrepreneur: the innovator, the calculating inventor, the over-optimistic promoter and the organization builder. These types are not related to the personality but rather the type of opportunity the entrepreneur faces.
- **Collins and Moore**—tough, pragmatic people driven by needs of independence and achievement. They seldom are willing to submit to authority.
- **Cooper, Woo & Dunkelberg**—argue that entrepreneurs exhibit extreme optimism in their decision-making processes.
- **John Howkins**—focused specifically on creative entrepreneurship. He found that entrepreneurs in the creative industries needed a specific set of traits, including the ability to prioritize ideas over data, to be nomadic and to learn endlessly.
- **David McClelland**—primarily motivated by an overwhelming need for achievement and strong urge to build.
- **Nathaniel "Nate" Couser/Operation Breakthrough Strategies Corporation**—highly motivated, being

able to take on unlimited challenges, able to accept full responsibility of his actions, highest level of determination, never accept failure as an option, extreme level of faith, unlimited persistence to achieve success, able to endure through any type of struggles, understand that the measure of success is of one's own measure and not the measure of others, and the ability to operate at the highest level of tenacity.

My entrepreneurial experience is varied and expansive. My extent of experience in entrepreneurship ranges from involvement with fortune 100 and 500 CEOs; successful Entrepreneurs and Small Business Owners of small, medium and large companies; Board and Advisory Board Members of major national to international procurement contracts; interaction with thousands of new and existing small business owners/entrepreneurs; extensive contract discussion issues with Government Officials and Advisors and participation in the White House Executive Offices to discuss important, current small business and large company topics to provide growth to our country.

I have also had the privilege of being presented as a success story to small businesses nationally by one of the largest small business financial forums in the world and by a national business procurement matching organization, along with support from one the largest chamber of commerce organizations. These accomplishments are not merely by chance or coincidence. Being supported by one of the largest Government Contractors in the world as a major sponsor to our consulting company, national small business perspective solutions company, has presented the largest

U.S. Government Contract Procurement ever awarded. This all was accomplished not by requesting, but by the actions and efforts of a successful small business solution.

I have been able to successfully establish over 1000 + "Teaming" relationships with top businesses in various segments across different industries to align with my first company's seven divisions in the first year of business. These "Teaming" relationships define the pinnacle of business relationships and resource building that have provided a great deal of success for our company as well as many others around the nation.

During my entrepreneurship quest, I have attracted and established an "Advisory Board" and formed relationships with well-established professionals, leaders (private, public, military), CEOs, Attorneys, prior Government Officials, celebrities, industry leaders, technology experts (marketing, financial, business, etc.), University Teaming relationships, leading officials of Universities and Non-Profit Organizations.

Entrepreneurs have to reach out to many sectors of business, including many resource sectors that are often invisible and not discussed at most conferences, seminars or national networking events.

Briefly, I believe that Entrepreneurs need to understand the roles of a Small Business Owner, CEO and President of a small business.

From speaking and working with thousands of entrepreneurs and small business owners over the past 5 years, we have found distinct differences in the mindsets and motivations of both entrepreneurs and small business owners. Take a look at the chart below to see some of the mindset differences:

Objectives & Views	Small Business Owner	Entrepreneur
1. Primary Motivation	To Make a Living	To Make an Impact and Significant Change
2. Personal Financial Goal	Regular Income	Exit Value of Company
3. Career Objective	Self-Employment	Financial Freedom
4. Financing Strategy	SBA or Bank Loans	Investors
5. Business Strategy	Creating More Sales	Providing Value
6. View of Assets	Real Estate and Inventory	Employees & Customers
7. Risk Taking Profile	Stability	Willing To Fail
8. Employee Compensation	Market Rate or Below	Will Pay for Top Talent
9. Work Environment	Extension of Owner's Home	Fast Paced and Growth Focused
10. Investment Profile	Main Investor/Owner of Company	Investor/ Involvement in Different Businesses
11. Daily Actions	Day-to-Day Manager	Strategy, Growth and Collaboration
12. Work Style	Long-Term and Enjoys Repetitive Tasks	Short-Term and a Serial Innovator/ Inventor

Entrepreneurship starts from God's driven journey customized especially for YOU!

I want to begin by saying that I am not trying to push any religious agenda on anyone. My journey of "Entrepreneurship," as well as many others, commence by faith and belief in God. My knowledge, wisdom and experiences are through my faith and direction in God for my life's journey. The second I reach any moment of anything I do in life is derived from God's ride for me as a passenger to him with God as the life driver. In other words, I ride with God and he drives my life, literally. Yes, I am human and yes, I have made many mistakes in life and long as I live, there will be many more mistakes. But I truly believe that once you are aligned with God's independent journey developed for each and every one of us, things align in life for the good.

Remember that things do not always work like we plan. Again, our lives are directed by God's plan. I always laugh inside when I hear people say they plan because even when I say I plan to accomplish something, it takes me back to the root of my life and I reflect back to what God has installed for me. While writing this book and going through my unplanned life experiences; they were totally unexpected, but God knew what I needed to experience in order to be able to write such a profound and supportive book. I can honestly say this was developed by me through God. My experience in life was developed this way to be able to reach as many business owners, entrepreneurs and people in general to provide a tremendous value to their lives in Entrepreneurship to help them be more knowledgeable in their quest for a long business or career journey.

It's funny how life reveals itself, but I always felt that I would be able to reach many professionals, entrepreneurs and people in general to provide a wealth of valuable information to help them in their business and career endeavors and just merely to add value as a whole in their everyday life activities.

I have provided a collaborated, self-opportunity of uniqueness as follows:

- Civilian career
- Military career
- Unique business experiences
- Personal skills
- Innovative Career traits
- Highly intelligent and Unique people in my life
- A true blessing of unlimited internal resources and abilities to be connected to people of true integrity, loyalty, knowledge, wisdom and value of life with the utmost fulfillment of innovative abilities.

The people who have gotten to know me have understood that I am and have always been a giving person, a person of always trying to do for others and a person of self-motivation.

It becomes a challenge in writing a book when life provides you with so much knowledge, wisdom and experiences that you want to share with many people to provide solutions, helpful skills, motivation, processes, methodologies and approaches to develop a success track of business and career. I never thought I would write a book, provide a platform for many professionals, business owners, entrepreneurs and coach and train people to save hundreds, thousands or even millions of dollars to provide better business processes. In my life, I have been blessed with so much great experience, spectacular knowledge, innovative, unique business methods and most importantly, great people to support my journey.

The fact is I have been blessed with so much knowledge, technical expertise, intelligence of business and wisdom and testimonies from a lifetime of experience that I have to create more than just this book to share this wealth of information. I will be publishing a complex "Technical" book to follow that will provide a more defined method of processes, methodologies and procedures that will provide "Fast Track" ways of accomplishing entrepreneurial business and career tracks for cost savings, time reduction and successful business practices for potentially winning various contracts. There has been much demand and an abundance of requests for me to develop a Book Series to highlight my uniquely designed methodology for understanding how to do business more successfully in the Government (Public) Sector Marketplace.

How am I able to evaluate these methods as being the most effective methodologies? They are measured by the following examples which have taken place in the last three years to the present, but have been in the making throughout my business and career experiences:

- Having the number one ranked, best Government Contractor as my Major Sponsor for "Operation Breakthrough Strategies—Small Business Platform" without even asking for their assistance.

- Having major law firms volunteer to be a support structure to my organizational platform without asking at no expense and providing a resource speaker and informational resource bank to my organization.

- Having major Heads of Government Agencies volunteer to be a support structure by speaking and being part of my small business platform.

- Having a major, national Business Credit Card company and national, small business procurement organization provide me as a success story, providing a full-time, organizational service of my "Teaming Knowledge" as a general, full-service, beginning program for business owners. These businesses have worked with me to create a national "Teaming" platform for national, functional small businesses and advertise me in their "Government Contracts—Victory in Procurement for Small Business—Insight Guide—OPEN FOR GOVERNMENT CONTRACTS," titled "Team to Help Win Government Contracts."

- Having this same, major national Business Credit Card Company comparing me as follows, **"Teaming Like A Pro"**—*"If teaming were a sport like basketball or golf, Nathaniel Couser would be on the level of Michael Jordan or Tiger Woods. Having built more than 400 formal teaming relationships in less than five years, Couser understands that partnerships mean more than simply looking out of own interest".*

And:

"If teaming were a sport like basketball or football, Nathaniel Couser would be on the level of Michael Jordan or Tom Brady. Having built more than 400 formal teaming relationships in less than five years, Couser understands that partnerships mean more than simply looking out of own interest".

Please note that the first quote was written prior to Tiger Woods' temporary downturn of success and the second quote was re-written to adequately describe my success story.

- Having Department of Defense (DOD) Officials take part in "Operation Breakthrough Strategies" as a support arm/ speaker and stating that they would like to endorse this platform to be a training and resource tool to provide as many small businesses nationally to complete as a certificate program or consulting program development. They could not legally do so, but just the idea of such a recommendation speaks volume of excellence! They wanted entrepreneurs and business owners to understand "How to do business with the Government" so that they would be better equipped with more effective business practices, methodologies and processes prior to coming to sell them services or products. They quoted that this would "save each and every Contracting Procurement Officer many thousands of dollars by spending more effective time with that small business because they would be more knowledgeable to understand what the Government Agencies' needs are and they would be equipped with the correct knowledge and presentation of high quality for their services and products."

- Informed by many small businesses that as I spoke in different parts of the country, they were able to implement what I said and now they have a successful business. Prior to hearing me speak, they were going to go out business until they implemented what I spoke about pertaining to some of our business processes of "Operation Breakthrough Strategies."

This is truly one of the reasons why a book of this nature needed to be written. Throughout the book, you will see why it was developed to help the many business and career people who need a little extra help.

As I reflect in this section and throughout the book, I have to discuss the topic of "Extraordinary." Namely, I want to talk about this subject matter because it is extremely impossible for this situation of innovativeness and uniqueness of methodology to be created which can be developed into one absolute platform. Such a platform like "Operation Breakthrough Strategies" had to be developed by an entire career, an aggressive entrepreneur process and a host of many supported companies of all types and sizes.

Some of the areas of concentration that make up this awesome business platform, entrepreneurial process and innovative methodology are as follows:

- Branding
- Business experience
- Contracting
- Creative strategies
- Determination

- Executive protection
- Innovation
- Logical thinking
- Multiple facets of consulting
- Marketing
- Persistence
- Procurement
- Strategic
- Teaming
- Technology
- Tenacity

Each and every one of us Entrepreneurs, Small Business Owners and Professionals have to fully and clearly understand that there is a path of business success for us as long as we define what is a demand versus detail niche in whichever industry we choose. In such a position, you have to fully understand that as you pursue your business success track, you have to maintain the highest integrity to accomplish success. You have to align your business with actual resources and people at every aspect along the way to support the innovative initiatives that match your targeted marketplace.

CREATION OF THE BOOK: From the beginning and throughout the creative process of me writing this book, my thoughts have remained clear and decisive with constant excitement, but accepting everyday changes in life's "cause-reaction," which continuously creates new and more challenging situations. This is what I call, the "Unexpected or Unpredicted." I still remain consistent, but continue to be flexible. My goals remain fixed, but shift to adapt and compensate to stay measured to my ultimate goal of success. Be cautious not to get caught up in the ever changing shift of success of the world. Stay consistent and steadfast in your faith-driven, laid-out path to what God precisely provides for you. Others around you can alter your goals, success and ultimately keep you on track. Sometimes they can take you entirely off base and cause your goals, successes to be completely diverted in another direction. To sum it up, "Stay on Course!"

Entrepreneurship starts from the value of self-determination and proper gathering of resources.

Through my journey of "Entrepreneurship," I have learned that it takes a person to their outer limits of self-drive, determination, motivation, tenacity, persistence, resourcefulness and most of all, in my arsenal of strategic tools, is "Faith." I know that there are many successful entrepreneurs in many different industries, but in my industry, "The Federal Government/Department of Defense," I decided to do my homework to succeed early in the journey of business ownership. I prepared myself for many years from early in life, including my childhood and Junior High school Years, to become the best Entrepreneur that I could be to keep up with both the demands of today and tomorrow's future. During my early years in junior high school I participated in sports, but not just one sport; I participated in Track & Field, Basketball, Football, Cross Country and even tried to play on two teams at one time. This to me was a true sign of entrepreneurship in the workings. While I participated in the sports, I held a part-time job and even tried to work two jobs so that I could accomplish more. My first job was a

Bag Boy, or Grocery clerk, as we call it now. While working this job part-time, I observed that others were content in their position and I was from day one trying to find out how I could advance, how I could get the manager's position, how I could make more money in a shorter period of time. And this was started from day 1. Throughout my junior high and high school years, I worked many jobs trying each time trying to figure out how to succeed, learning how I could do it better, but learning as many processes as I could to build a more robust experience. During the school year, while going to practice after school, I took it upon myself to practice in the early mornings before school. Then after practice, I went to work at my part-time job, and then went home to have family time, homework, and start the next day all over again. This was my weekly routine and on the weekends, I explored my entrepreneurial journey by spending a lot of time on the military bases and with my grandfather retrieving all of the military knowledge I could gather and enjoying his mentorship. Between my Father working on NASA's facility, my Mother working at a hospital and relatives returning from the Vietnam War, I experienced the presence of Government aligned with Langley Air Force Soldiers, Fighter Squad Commands taking flight, troops at Fort Eustis, troops at Fort Monroe, Navy Sailors, Coast Guard & Marines at various area Navy Bases and Weapons Stations. I had first-hand knowledge and exposure to Government Contracting. I asked many questions, observed and of course, elected to spend my schooling and career dedicated to the Military and Government, blended with private sectors. This provided a great value to the start of my pursuit as an Entrepreneur. My calling to be an Entrepreneur was driven from a young age, it goes back further than I can even remember. I always wanted to be the one to run a company, but resolutely making certain to share the process and rewards with others. You see, I thought in my early days that you always have to have someone with you to achieve success. A great mind can independently think of the great innovativeness for today and tomorrow, but align other minds collectively in the same path of success and nothing will be unachievable.

This book is not about my childhood. However, I wanted to provide various milestones in my life as I re-visit my journey to entrepreneurship so that it may help many other rising entrepreneurs, seasoned entrepreneurs and youth that are seeking to become entrepreneurs. I think that it is important for everyone to understand that entrepreneurship starts at a very early age. Throughout my entire career, prior to stepping out as a fully committed entrepreneur, I noticed that every job I worked, even if the job was great, I was still missing something. I was always searching for something else to enhance the job or I would have additional ideas that would make it better. This to me was truly a sign of entrepreneurship.

As I worked through many jobs, consulting assignments, contract assignments, I noticed a trend. The trend was that I would be hired to do one thing, and then asked to take on many other assignments, but of course for the same pay. But I did not mind because it was taking me to my ultimate destination of "Entrepreneurship." While working on any particular job, I noticed that there was nothing that I could not accomplish because of my level of determination and ability to find whatever resource I needed to accomplish the job. I can remember many times working on a job and I was asked if I knew how to perform that particular task, and of course, I said yes, knowing I had no clue. However, I was confident that I would figure it out in a very short time or get up to speed with it prior to commencement of the task.

The great value of a supportive spouse can generate a true path to success.

Throughout the normal human tests and trials in the life of entrepreneurship, a supportive spouse, friend or support person and in my case, my Beautiful Wife (Stephanie) has and will continue to bring the outer limits of valued support. I can only explain a small part of her huge, heroic support with little words because she has exerted and exuded more than words can explain. You know we all go through life striving for a supportive spouse and I can say in my lifetime, I have received the God given gift of a supportive Wife. It doesn't have to be just the large things that she continues to provide support for, but it is the small, intangible things that normally yield so much reward that her support counters any negativity.

My Wife provides so much support that it drives my desire to succeed in an un-measureable desire. She feels my pains, happiness and desires to help others through my pursuit of entrepreneurship. She is always there for me even if we are many miles away from each other. During the many successes and downfalls of life's journey, I reach deep in my spiritual support structure and I can always count on my Wife's support. She is always there for me filling the desire in my heart. Her love for me illustrates the power to succeed, overcome, see light in the darkest times and provide inner strength in me that is completely unexplainable.

Regardless of the huge obstacles in my way, she provides me with a will to succeed. In other words, she provides me with unlimited power to succeed. I could write a book just on a "Supportive Wife in the Pursuit of Entrepreneurial Success." Maybe that will come later! I am truly blessed to have come through my lifetime with such a magnificent Wife. Even while having such great support from my Wife, I have received myriad blessings from having such great children and a wonderful grandchild. I look so forward to growing old with my Wife, Children and Grandchild. Again, as I mentioned above about writing a book on my Wife, I could write a book on my children, as well. They should be highly noticed and recognized as role models for successful children, not just by their academic achievements or their successful career paths, but their values as adults.

Praise the Lord! Thank God for my journey!

What I am about to tell you in this book, will and should change lives. These are true events that occurred and these events are only mentioned in this book to provide other entrepreneurs with valuable tools, weapons and information to overcome whatever they set out to accomplish in their quest for success. It will hopefully provide an inspiration to succeed in their business venture.

I will start this book by mentioning the importance of special people such as **my Wife, my Children, my Parents, Grandchild, my True Friends and other Professionals/Supporters** that I surround myself with throughout my life and align with my character. Keep in mind that throughout your journey, "True Friends" will be there consistently through your successes, but most importantly, through your hardest struggles. Whatever you do, please stand your ground, stay firm to your "Faith" and push along your long journey to achieve your measured success. Further along in the book, I will get more detailed about your measured success.

My Wife

My Wife is a very special and beautiful, blessed lady of the greatest integrity, loyalty, supportiveness, faith and has true direction and drive. She demonstrates the true definition of a "wife" in ways that I can truly say make day-to-day life occurrences and business ventures go much smoother. Whether things are at their highest or lowest, she supports me 100% regardless of whether she thinks that I am in left field, too far to the right or just right on my ideas. Her integrity is of a rare breed that in many ways define the true values needed to support her husband. These include indescribable details that provide me with a strong foundation of supportive strength from a spouse, a true best friend, a woman of balance and exceptional family values and character.

My wife has to have great faith to be married to an Entrepreneur like me because sometimes being an entrepreneur can be one of the toughest careers that there are in life. She illustrates faith in God like no other that takes us to the untapped limitations of God's blessings.

My opinion is that you have to have this alignment to succeed merely just in life itself. Even in times of great despair, she shows greater faith than when we are on high-achieving visits to the White House, or being awarded multi-million to multi-billion dollar contracts, or receiving an award of achievement for running this business, or working late hours and putting up with me when the lights are on in our bedroom from late night to sunrise or for never-ending let-downs such as knowing this is the day of contract success when it is really three years later.

I could write a book just merely on her faith as a strong woman in Christ. My Wife, in my thought, is truly blessed in the Lord in ways that reflect her character, her way of dealing consistently with people, in general, each and every day. There have been times when people have done her wrong, but she chooses to stay focused on her consistent way of treating people kindly in the most difficult of times. In her walk with God, she radiates through people, providing them a comfort of assurance which she defines through the goodness and prosperity of being blessed.

My wife has a great direction and drive for family values that extend far beyond the usual, traditional ways. She travels in a path of life that places God first, which lays a platform for sequential planning of success through personal demonstrations. My Wife is my support structure and brings unlimited value to my balance of entrepreneurship and quest for success as I measure it in my life.

Based on my unexpected occurrences, my Wife has illustrated immeasurable support that without would cause the average, actually above average person, into a straight pathway to failure and where most would settle and choose to remain.

As I wrote this book, my Wife was unaware of the changes I was going through emotionally, but was saddled with her own emotions as we traveled through this challenging journey of entrepreneurship together. You see, "entrepreneurship" as we are told, is not just merely an individual journey, but requires a test of your truest Faith of Spouses, Friends and Enemies to stand with you or leave you in the hardest times. My Wife—My Best Friend—My Support Structure—My Resources Bank—My Vision—My Heart—My Companion—My Soul-Mate—My Everything!

Results of successful and exceptional children being produced bring confirmation for multiple business achievement as well as great parenting.

I have experienced a great deal of joy through my parenting situation. I was involved in a previous marriage that did not work out at the end, but even then, the platform for raising our children provided a great success track. We exposed our children to all diversified situations so that their values would be exceptional in the way of them being productive citizens in our country.

My oldest son, Natario, or Dr. Couser, has an undergraduate degree in Biochemistry and his Medical Degree in Optometry. I had my son practically as a kid myself. Natario was and still remains a great role model to his siblings. Natario, as a small kid, decided he wanted to be a doctor, be a person to help others, be a person that puts others before himself. This was a success story in the making and we worked to guide and protect him for a path to that success. His goals were so ambitious as a small child that they filtered down to his younger brother and sister. Natario is making a difference for many others in society. **Natario's Wife, Deanna or Dr. Couser,** of Anesthesiology and **their Son** and **Our Grandson (Tyce Isaiah)** are also great sources of inspiration.

My youngest son, Taurice, has an undergraduate degree in Kinetic Imagery. He is now a successful Small Business Owner who develops advanced programming, animation, Xbox & IOS games and Mobile Apps along with other games for various gaming systems. Taurice had a dream. Carrying his art pad around as a young kid everywhere, and now as an adult, he is living out his dream. Taurice has always been a great kid and now an awesome adult making a difference in this country educating and providing mobility and agility functioning capabilities through his gaming products.

My oldest daughter, Fallyn Gray, has an undergraduate degree in Public Policy, Management and Development with an emphasis in Urban Planning and Development. Fallyn has always been a great communicator which has led her to her position as a Vice President for one of the largest United States' Banks supervising over 30 plus professionals located in Dallas, TX and Denver, CO. She has always played a role in the community and now participates in several community organizations as a participant and leader.

My youngest daughter, Crystal, has an undergraduate degree through the College of Humanities and Social Sciences in Psychology. Crystal has passionately worked for about two years helping autistic children, and now she is a University Counselor considering Law School. She enjoys life and has a great determination to succeed and it was amplified when there was a time in her life where she was at a death's door.

In November 2008, as My Wife, Stephanie, and I traveled to Washington, D. C. by request of a Department of Homeland Security representative, Dan, to participate in a great event which would be a great success to add to my portfolio and relationship building. Like many other trips from my home here in Dallas, TX to Washington, D. C., I normally always planned to go by and spend time with my son and daughter while in town.

This particular trip was very odd for me. It was odd because the trip was last minute, with a quick turn back. Having limited time, I planned to revisit my daughter the next weekend by surprise, but I never would've expected the surprise we would encounter on that chilly day in November.

The plan was for my Wife and I to leave on late Saturday afternoon for the event with Dan and travel to New York on Sunday morning for more meetings, end on Monday and back to Dallas, TX to potentially travel to Dubai.

Well, as we approached the Baltimore-Washington Airport, I received a call from my ex-wife, Patricia. She stated that our daughter, Crystal, had been in a car accident and by the grace of God, we just happened to be in the area about 25 minutes away from the hospital they were taking my daughter. As we approached the rental car drop-off ramp, we immediately re-routed to a direct rapid drive to the hospital.

Shortly afterwards, I received a call from my Son, Dr. Couser, that he was at the hospital and the doctors told him that they had approximately 45 minutes or so to save my daughter's life. I strategically tried to get to her. As I prayed, a nurse was pushing a stretcher down the hall rushing this pale skinned lady to surgery trying to save her life.

My Wife said to me, "I think that is Crystal." I replied, no because this lady is of a different nationality; she is too light-skinned. As the lady got closer, I realized that my wife was correct; it was my little princess. I looked over her with great despair and she looked up into my eyes and said, "Dad, how did you get here so quick from Texas?" It was almost as she was unaware of her life-threatening condition.

I told her to pray like no day ever before. Do not concentrate on anything else but living for God and she would succeed to live another day. My Princess had more than just one life threatening injury, but through God, she was graced with the blessing to continue to live.

Stephanie and I automatically decided that we were not going anywhere until Crystal, My Princess, was ready to leave the hospital. We were told that it would take about 6-8 months before she would be well enough to leave the hospital.

Through Faith and Prayers, Crystal fast-tracked through two hospitals and one acute rehabilitation hospital by the Grace of God and her will to live. She successfully achieved release from the hospital in about 30 days total. Crystal left the hospital in a wheelchair, continued rehab and was recommended to forego school for the remainder of the semester.

Crystal, determined like me, decided that she wanted to return to school in January 2009. She returned to school, minus one of her friends that passed away beside her in the accident, to achieve continued academic success. Crystal's University President provided great support and accommodation for Crystal to return to college in a supportive way like no other.

Crystal now maintains life in a stronger and clearer vision of its importance and is doing great on her pathway to success. I present this story to you in my entrepreneur book because again, there will be many obstacles, walls, struggles and adversity. And my recommendation is to stick to your faith and stay consistent in your pursuit of entrepreneurial success. Your strength to succeed should be God, Spouse, Children and your closest true friends.

Parents' wisdom and their struggles demonstrate results of an Entrepreneur.

As parents ourselves, along with our parents and others' parents, we all play a vital role in our success as an Entrepreneur. Not only do we build our character towards entrepreneurship, but we lend great value in our thinking towards our continued journey of the world of business. A lot of us entrepreneurs tend to address problems from a standpoint of an enclosed bubble because as we travel down that road of entrepreneurship, we understand from our business predecessors that you should keep a lot to yourself which is partially true.

The reason: while working partially out of the bubble, in a sense, you have to think "protection" while in the trenches of business. Our Parents tend to have always tried to form a source of protection as we grew up to be productive adults which is great, but sometimes it can be a handicap to our entrepreneurship.

We must analyze what is positive and negative from our parents and create a written or mental model of their wisdom as it pertains to business and everyday life so that we can build an internal and external information bank. From having the honor of being around great CEOs, Entrepreneurs and Executives, I have witnessed first-hand shared stories, testimonies and tremendous adversity they have had to overcome. This has provided me with great wisdom. I have had the opportunity to hear stories passed down from their parents which provided an additional level of strategic building tools of information.

Our parents play a role in our arsenal as an entrepreneur that can provide a long-term source of valuable information towards our goals and avoidance of our failures.

Our friends we align ourselves with reflect positive or negative results to impact entrepreneurship.

Business has unique characteristics and our friends' characteristics can play a vital role to the success or drastic failure. A lot of times, we hold our friendships to the highest caliber, but in the "life of business," we have to go many extra steps further.

After being in business for myself for over 5 years and having my career centered around business for over 20 plus years, I have heard all kinds of stories, negative and positive. But after experiencing very devastating situations relating to friends, business partners and family, I would tell you to be VERY careful in your alignment of who you choose to place as positive people around you.

The more success achieved, the more positive and negative attraction you will receive from others. At the birth of your business, friends will be by your side and the opposition or fake friends will be even closer. You have to create a "Check

& Balance" system that analyzes and evaluates your friends periodically. For your opposition and fake friends, you should analyze them continuously, day-to-day.

In your creation of a "Check & Balance" system, you should develop a system that will provide a continuous, cyclic structure of character, trust, loyalty and other attributes to be measured so that you do not fall into an ill-guided venture of friendship. As an example, here is a minimized list of system testing measures:

FRIENDS	FAKE FRIENDS/ OPPOSITION
Continuously check loyalty.	Always check their intentions.
Measure trust by information.	Release test information.
Provide general direction of business early to check their opinions of your business as related to potential profit.	Provide general direction of business early to check their opinions of your business as related to potential profit.
Discuss fragmented informational part(s) of the business to check to see what type of questions they will be most concerned about related to your business.	Discuss fragmented informational part(s) of the business to check to see what type of questions they will be most concerned about related to your business.
Maintain control of releasing information about your business until absolutely sure they are near 100% supportive of your business.	Release limited information about your business until absolutely sure they are close to 100% supportive of your business.

Based on my experience and many other Business Owners, CEOs, Entrepreneurs and Presidents, you have to be very strategic in releasing information to anyone about your business, including friends and "want-to-be-friends (WTBF.)" True "longevity-committed friends (LCF)" will provide almost instant assurance of loyalty without having to second guess their intentions. But people that have bad intentions about your business one way or the other will provide initial "flags of failure (FAF)" fairly quickly through visual or verbal cues.

Bad intentions, by experience, normally come in many forms. A brief list to name a few:

- A strong willingness to ask many questions about your business, but they do not provide any information to you about their business.
- Very aggressive about immediate friendship and early commitment with you in business.
- Very aggressive about your business and how it should perform.
- Overbearing with their kindness to help you in your business.
- Very aggressive on conducting business with you before they get to know you.
- Very aggressive strictly on monetary values alone, but really don't concern themselves with the business process.
- Not apprehensive at all on wanting to partner prior to understanding the character and direction of each other's business.
- Extremely loud talking and having to be the one heard in the entire room.
- Extremely difficult to deal with in a non-business environment.

- In a restaurant environment, have the waiter or waitress intentionally mess up the meal order of the person wanting to do business with you to see how they react to the situation. If they react cordially, then you have an inkling that they are somewhat stable. However if they become partial to egregious or disrespectful behaviors, then immediately shutdown this potential business arrangement.

The bad intentions mentioned above are merely limited measures that can be used to accomplish the alignment of positive friends and business associates. There are many other "rules of measurement (ROM)" to achieve great relationships in business and to reveal quickly unaligned relationships that will more than likely cause business failure.

Whatever you do to align great friendships in your business, never second guess yourself and never use a quick method of approval to align true friends in your entrepreneurial journey. Most people will not understand your business direction initially, so judge your alignment strategically by at least a "Three Check System (TCS)" of approval. As mentioned earlier in the book and many more times throughout, carefully and slowly take your time to invest in a minimum of 3 times to check and re-check every aspect of your business relationships. If not the first time, even the second time you may find yourself not finding any failures of the relationship, but then the 3rd time will normally reveal the immediate "failure of alignment (FOA.)" After all checks, always have a final analysis and review as to what decision you decide after the "Three Check System (TCS.)"

PART III

THE TRADITIONAL WAY... MOST FAILURES OF SMALL BUSINESSES!

THE PROCESS OF SMALL BUSINESS PENETRATION!

UNDERSTANDING GOVERNMENT CONTRACTING, NOT FOLLOWING TRADITION TO FAILURE!

BREAKING BARRIERS, OBSTACLES AND ADVERSITY!

Chapter 3

Breaking the Barriers in Government & Private Sector Contracting

Providing help along the way to others to build a broadened team.

My philosophy of helping, supporting and collaborating with others, which I describe in much greater detail throughout this book, is based on the vital principles of an innovative method that has been proven in many different industries by my entrepreneurial practices short of a half decade. I had an opportunity to experiment with this innovativeness over twenty-five years of my professional military and private sector career developing, implementing, managing and executing contracts.

Since the beginning of pursuing my career, I always had a built-in strategy of helping others to achieve their ambitions while reaching for my own ambitions. Throughout my military career, I had numerous opportunities to develop a one-track, independent success story for myself, but I chose to bring others on the success ride along with me. I have always felt that the more people you help when the opportunity lends itself, you bring together an unstoppable team of excellence. Your success level will rise to a greater level, this time with more support power.

My belief of business is based on winning by "Teaming." The only way to create a great team is to do for others and in return, the right people of integrity will do for you. You can provide many resources to support and help others while pursuing your business journey. The resources will define a common business bond around unity of one complete team. I know because I have accumulated over 1000 teaming partners in a two-year period merely by helping one another.

Here are a few resources that can be very useful in helping others to create a great team:

- When someone asks you a question, don't just answer, but explain in greater content.
- Provide ample time to listen to others when they need to explain things to you about their business ideas.
- Keep an open communication line to others that you feel will make a great team member.
- Often, a person may not initially have much to offer to you in terms of resource information, but don't let that be the decision to not support them.
- Never expect something in return just because you provide information to others.
- Always respect others and their opinions even when you don't agree.

- Be truthful to others regardless of whether or not it appeals to them.
- Look for the greatest in individuals no matter whether their appearance meets your expectations.
- Define a person by their character and loyalty, not by their worth.
- Provide continuous meetings between both of you to build a great relationship.

Creation of Innovativeness

Every business may be different based on industry, sources and results, but generally all businesses will use some of the same techniques, approaches, processes and methodologies. Actually all businesses should be utilizing typical business tools, but most do not implement any complete techniques. They don't define the proper approach to any measure of the business alignment which leads to total lack of process. Therefore, the methods to be utilized can become null and void.

Working with the right company by means of a common interest in all avenues will be True **"OBT Strategic Teaming™"** and Partnering. This is the strongest creation of innovativeness for entrepreneurial success in breaking barriers in Government and private sector contracting. My entrepreneurial success, business model of success and the system logic of business were accomplished by my creation of a methodology that we call **"OBT Strategic Teaming™."** Our creative methodology is designed by way of success for 2 or more businesses collectively benefitting by means of each other's resources and most importantly, their success of winning contracts by means of a complete building structure. There is never one company that achieves success solely by themselves despite what you may hear. This means that breaking barriers to win government contracts is never done alone in a vacuum. This is the downfall of most small businesses thinking that they can win contracts by themselves. Government contracting takes quite a bit of series of single-track, multiple complex branches of structure and systems to achieve barrier breakthrough. Private sector is similar, but contain much more simplified, single branches of structure and far less confusion, barriers, obstacles, adversity and systems of complexity.

Innovation is very important in creating a unique system of business operation. **"Generation Collaborative Breakthrough (GCB)"** is a technique created and used by Operation Breakthrough Strategies Corporation creator Nate Couser which is highly vital in any company's approach. Plan for both now and the future with new generated technology, **OBT Teaming for Credibility™ (OBTTFC™)** and collaborated teaming approach.

Your most effective support arm will be stronger through the commitment of relationships by way of teaming along with combined resources. Again, most small businesses do not accomplish the success of winning contracts because they lack the creation of innovativeness. Most innovative creations require sharing, trust and the ability to truly team. This is one of the main reasons why most small businesses lack innovative creations due to the lack of sharing fairly and lack of trust due to thinking that they should be accomplishing success by themselves.

"Stimulated Innovative Growth (SIG)" is another creative innovativeness that is vitally important in understanding government contracting. Always think outside of the box for forecasted research, growth and precise targeted expansion of business tools (Approaches, Methodologies, Procedures, Processes, Cycles, Culture, Economics, Standards, Techniques, etc.)

When we as small businesses get to the top of success, we will want to be teamed with others because the challenge gets much greater and complicated at the top, but most importantly, it makes life much easier in the entrepreneurial journey because **OBT Teaming by Credibility™** accomplishes more than you can imagine. When striving to the top of success, you want to be with someone you can trust, build a strong relationship with and who truly understands the logic of teaming. Or at least they should be willing to learn and implement true teaming.

Understanding the Process
(Certifications help but not the solution.)

Government Contracting is a Series of Business Processes, intervention of techniques, relationship of collaboration, complex method of contracting, unlinking methodology and complex procurement cycle—it is not a one cycle process.

Government procurement in the United States that supports CONUS and OCONUS locations addresses the federal government's need to acquire goods, services and interests in real property. It involves acquiring by contract, usually with appropriated funds, supplies, services and interests in real property by and for the use of the

Federal Government through a purchase or lease. It can vary on whether the supplies, services or interests are already in existence or must be created, developed, researched, demonstrated and evaluated. When in an acquisition form of procurement, it is defined as to goods and services only. Federal Government Contracting has the same elements as contracting between private parties: a lawful reason, competent contracting parties, an offer (based on best value or best price), an acceptance that complies with the terms of the offer, mutuality of obligation and consideration. But Federal contracts are subject to volumes of statutes dealing specifically with Federal contracts and the Federal contracting process, most of which can be found in the United States Code. In short, while the fundamental theoretical constraints of Federal contracting and contracting between private parties are the same, Federal contracting is much more heavily regulated and complex.

- A Process "Operation Breakthrough Strategies™ (OBS™)" of how to figure out during business with the Government/ Public and Private Sector. A unique approach of performing business to win contracts, save money, maximum marketing and business resources at little to no expense, but limited vested time sent to accomplish goals.
- Mindset—prior to seeking out Government Agencies to inquire about business, be prepared, know "how and what" value you are bringing to the Agency. Understand "why" you should fit into their equation of business and when the timing is right.

Certifications are great to have in your business model and structure, but have them with a purpose of benefit for your business.

Keep in mind that a certification is a "License to Hunt **(LTH)**" and "Permit to be in Attendance **(PBA)**" and has no position to allow contract wins. There is a myth by most small business owners/ entrepreneurs that most certifications in Government contracting is seen as a high privilege. They arrive at this assumption from conferences, seminars and the industry because it is indirectly stated that certain certifications will allow for contract wins. There are various consulting and service oriented companies that translate this to small business owners/entrepreneurs because they truly believe this can happen. It is usually false, but can be true in some cases. There are rare circumstances where some small businesses can achieve contract success with added certifications. This can only take place if there is a serious niche driven contract for that particular small business with a particular needed product or service that may be in great demand by an agency or large company.

There is mostly false hope on merely getting contracts by obtaining certifications alone because it involves many steps in a well-defined business structure to be achieved.

Certifications should be like an overlay of support with many interlinking layers of structure combined with inner methodologies that allows outer results of successful processes to setup contract "Positioning of Success **(POS.)**" Certifications should be linked as an outer layer of embedded strategies that provide a "Connection of Communication **(COC)**" to your client base by means of direct or indirect relationship of "Forward Collaborated Intelligence **(FCI.)**"

Understanding Government Contracting entails a very sophisticated art of complexity, but can be accomplished with a precise "System of Structure **(SOS.)**" There are many ways to accomplish great success in Government Contracting, but it will take a lot of work, endurance, patience, array of strategies and an abundance of resources. Don't be misguided and believe that you can accomplish Government Contracting by just merely chasing a contract, (i.e. like a dog chasing its tail), you have to really do your homework, define your destiny and clarify your path of success as to what it will take to get you there.

Here are a few, initial, key strategies for creating your structure:

- Form relationships that will be beneficial for contracting pursuit.
- Form teaming relationships that can bring benefit to others.
- Utilize "Competitive Forward Intelligence **(CFI)**" to forecast your business logic to define greater advancement of information.
- When developing your plan of pursuit for contracting, always define your path of least resistance and greater fluidity.
- Always think forward to plan for the present state of your structure.

This is just a few initial key strategies of many that construct a complete structure as indicated by our **OBTS Structure Model™ (OBTSSM™.)**

Remember, to be successful in anything you set out to do in life, you have to completely understand it and develop the entire process to accomplish it. This is the same with Government Contracting. This is not an overnight task, it's a journey that many small business owners/entrepreneurs take and the successful ones take time to develop a complete structure. Take the right journey of success.

Planning properly for the Federal Marketplace & Private Sector.

My advice to all Small Business Owners and Entrepreneurs: be very precise, technical, detailed, clearly defined and strategic in your planning process of business pursuit in the Federal Marketplace and Private Sector. One proven method of planning that we have implemented in our business planning process is known as "Proper Planning Prevents Poor Pursuit or Performance" (6P's or PPPPPP.)

We define one of our known processes by breaking it down in sequential order of the OBTS planning structure of the Six Ps (Proper Planning Prevents Poor Pursuit or Performance):

- Proper: Be very accurate in gathering the correct resources, information and associated participants in your business.
- Planning: Define your method(s) of accomplishing your mission. Be very clear in your diagrams, maps, charts and layouts of strategic information.
- Prevent: At all costs, avoid the mistakes of others. Review case studies, speak with successful and unsuccessful business owners and do not implement hypothetical situations from what you may hear from others. Always clarify unknown facts.

- Poor: Do not accept less than the equal value of excellence. Always strive for the highest standards of achievement.
- Pursuit: Don't follow traditional failed practices, lead and follow fact-proven practices.
- Performance: Execute and follow through with the greatest commitment to achieve no less than excellence. Aim high and push higher!

In your proper planning process, you need to fully understand your place in the Federal Marketplace and Private Sector. Both of these market segments follow the same planning processes, but in the Federal Marketplace there are various situations where you have to follow different rules of engagement:

Proper Planning in the Federal Marketplace:

- Never plan your pursuit by means of doing it all yourself. All businesses that reach success plan for others in their business planning. A large amount of failed businesses planned their pursuit of business by themselves with no supporting teaming members, partners or associated businesses. This happens when small business owners think that they either need to do it themselves because they will lose revenue or just merely do not understand the importance of proper planning.
- Obtain facts from industry successes and implement processes only by confirmation of supported resources already tested by the marketplace.

Proper Planning in the Private Sector:

* You can plan your pursuit with limited support. It is still best to work with others in your planning process because you can gain many competitive resources and cut costs in your pursuit.
* You should always plan with precision, but you can follow others' success because of lesser rules of engagement.
* Planning can be less complex and can be accomplished in a shorter time span because the laws are not driven by the Federal Acquisition Regulations which can be very cumbersome by nature of the depth of each regulation.

Make **"Planning a Priority (PAP)"** in your initial development and your planning model will be directed toward the path of success. Develop the intricate parts of your roadmap to be totally based on the foundations of planning. Implement the process flow with the steps of collaborated planning cycles and execute the complete planning model once you have embedded all the aspects of proper planning.

There is a reason for the season for your Business. Find your season by researching your marketplace thoroughly to provide a great reason for your business to be a great benefit to the marketplace. Save yourself a great deal of money by spending a significant amount of time to ensure that all planning procedures are thoroughly vetted and all facts are used toward building your planning model.

There is an understanding in the Federal Marketplace that Government Contracting is very confusing. It is also fully understood that doing business with the Government is very difficult. Well, it is extremely difficult because within the industry, communication at conferences and seminars, the literature for Government Contracting has huge gaps. This means there is no synergy between segments of the Government Contracting process. On various occasions, there is an opportunity to bring a better understanding on "How to do Business with the Federal Government." But it is often suppressed by the overwhelming source of directional information driven by all aspects of business, except the most important source, which should be directed by "Small Business Successors (SBS)" of the marketplace. As you can see, it is very difficult to develop a successful planning process when your base information has many gaps and misguided information that come from Government Agencies and Large Companies that don't provide sequential order to the small business process. Therefore, the small businesses come away from the Conferences, Seminars, Symposiums and other instructional sessions simultaneously excited and confused more than ever. Wouldn't it be easier to get a sequential order of critical business information for understanding Government Contracting from other successful small businesses by more in depth collaboration at these type events? Without a proper order of business functionality directed to the small businesses, a tremendous amount of business failures plague the Federal Marketplace. Check out the statistical numbers to see the continuous number of small businesses going out of business by the hundreds and even thousands.

In order to really highlight your true planning outline with a combined parallel functionality, you have to conceptually obtain the untold story or the non-existent business process of doing business with the Federal Government. The untold story is the solution for actually doing business with Government correctly and the complete planning model that provides a business planning cycle from beginning to end.

As entrepreneurs/small business owners seek to gather vital information at conferences and seminars to build their planning model, they realize that there is no relative substance at these events that take them to an order of sequence. Even where there is important literature distributed, there is no information that can truly show them how to do business from say levels 101 to 501. Entrepreneurs/Small Business Owners are informed that at the general conferences or breakout sessions that these levels are taught, but this is not the case. There is a tremendous gap that will be discussed later in Chapter 7.

There is no strategic process as to how Entrepreneurs & Small Business Owners can create an overall sequential development of order for success in Government Procurement & Contracting because there is non-existence of an "End-to-End" set of solutions or platforms available among the industry at conferences, workshops, seminars and other events by Government Agencies.

To make your entrepreneurial business journey easier when planning for your pursuit, please do your "homework." You may be the most talented Entrepreneur/Small Business Owner in your market industry, but by not doing your due diligence or not properly developing a strategic plan of action, you will ensure immediate failure.

Positioning for Balance (Financial Planning)

When creating your strategic position for the launch of your financial planning, always ensure that you fully understand your business as it relates to today and where it fits in the future. Always wholeheartedly believe that your business will be successful 100%. This is crucial because when you are ready to approach investors, you must make certain they both believe in and fully understand your business before you get them engaged in your business. The investors need to understand the success paths of your business and most importantly, the failures that can obstruct your business success. Your ideas are what makes the success of your business and the investors' money is purely a resource which they benefit from by your business success. Don't let money change or rule your ideas. Your success will overcome all obstacles and types of adversity if you plan properly. Always execute every planning aspect of your business by precision of accurate calculations.

Here are some important factors for positioning for balance financially when planning and implementing the need of investors, bank financing and other funding support:

- At the inception of your business, always start and continue with intermittent sourcing of a licensed CPA.
- Keep detailed and accurate financial records.
- Keep your business expenses separate from your personal expenses.
- Absolutely keep all envelopes, packages and materials from all business credit cards, loan papers, etc.
- Make sure all financial agreements are produced through legal representation.

- Make certain that all financial matters are known within your business by 3 or more professionals.
- Check, double and triple check all financial decisions prior to making them.

Economically, always know where your business fits into your specific industry type and strategically know how others are positioned in the industry as well. Research to find out how others have positioned financially to bring a strategic balance into their business models. Always develop a process of due diligence to achieve a complete positioning balance. A Small Business/ Entrepreneur should figure out how to effectively work with a Government agency, medium and large companies and even other small businesses to advance themselves to success. Strategic Tip: Small Business Owners/Entrepreneurs should offer free support services to medium and large companies to better understand the financial process of business. The host of services should be to help them at no cost by adding support to their existing staff. This will help you learn through real-time experience and bring a better strategic positioning for your business. This is what I call "Additive Intelligence Tool (AIT)" for gaining knowledge without paying for it. Yes, you give up time, but the wealth of experience will have much greater valuable than you could even buy.

By fulfilling these services, at a minimum you will gain a substantial amount of "Strategic Knowledge Positioning (SKP)" as follows:

- You gain an unofficial mentoring-to-protégé source of knowledge.

- You gain a great deal of financial experience which allows greater "Intelligent Awareness Positioning (IAP.)" You creatively gain current, real-time experience to achieve more favorable strategic placement.
- You gain better financial skills for your employees.
- You gain additional resources for your business structure.
- You gain additional and stronger relationships.
- Most of all, you benefit from a form of "Innovative Small Business Resources" known as "Teaming!"

Always seek to achieve certifications and creatively concentrate on unique certifications to add more value to your positioning business model. Ensure that your certifications are in line with your overall business model. Create a "Strategic Alignment of Positioning (SAP)" to separate yourself from your competitors. Ultimately, you should collaborate with your competitors to be partners for the future.

Don't rely just on organizations to help your business growth.

While it is a great value to create a combined set of relationships with other businesses, organizations, committees and other entities to achieve innovative ways of collaboration, it is of great importance to isolate yourself from dependency. The majority of small businesses do not understand the importance of "True Teaming" which prevents them from becoming too dependent on others. The dependency grows in their lack of business structure and this creates a tremendous potential for failure.

Remember, it is not the responsibility of other organizations to help your business grow. It is to your advantage to create a need of reliance of other organizations to support your business's quest for growth.

This will provide numerous innovative growth strategies as follows:

- Initial business structure is built in many areas: *business, finance, management, training, resources, etc.*
- Base structure definition to support your financial model.
- Branding and marketing for credibility.
- Resource bank for knowledge.

It is very important in the Government marketplace to rely on other organizations for indirect support over direct support. Some indirect support as follows:

- Analyze and coordinate with others in their methods of success by interaction at events, symposiums, seminars and other informational events. Do not count on support at a conference unless it has informational sessions.
- Case studies are a great way to review success patterns which you can depend upon in business.
- Review 10K Reports for public companies.
- Review Annual & Financial Reports for private companies.
- Analyze and review factual information from reliable resources.
- Gather 3, 5 and 10-year trend reports if available along with projected goals.

- After performing your due diligence of interested companies for support, always get to know the entire leadership of the company from a personal standpoint and by extremely detailed business traits *(i.e. get to know all aspects of the person before you commit to an informal or formal relationship.)*

Traditional failures of small businesses are contingent upon a lack of reliance of working relationships with others. There are many ways to penetrate the traditional failures of small businesses by implementing several processes as follows:

- Always form relationships based on trusted sources, not monetary reasons.
- Always proceed with facts, not potentials.
- Always operate from mutual trust, don't accept less.
- Don't assume that because you have certifications that you are validated for an immediate business relationship.
- Don't allow yourself to form a relationship because the other business or organization has great success. Get to know the character and attributes behind the success of the source leadership.

Don't rely on organizations to help your growth, but rely on their successes to build your foundation of structure. Collect their failures to construct a strong and extensive list of things that you will not repeat in business. By implementing these techniques, you will develop a strong resolve to break through the barriers of Government business. You will create innovative ways to counter obstacles and to overcome adversities. But this is just the beginning.

Sustaining success

Naturally, we all have to gain success to sustain it, but it all starts with the business foundation generated with interlinking structural support. What does this mean? Well, every business must formalize a multi-functional, multi-source bank of countermeasures to react to struggles that come in your path. Based on the history of business, there will be struggles in the forms of *Adversity, Defeat, Disappointment, Let-down, Failure, Obstacles, Oversight and Setbacks.* I can attest to these unplanned events of the business journey because I have lived through it on my road to setback and success. Every business will go through its course of struggles. No business will succeed without simultaneously building structure while generating strategies. Success will only be achieved by breaking through the barriers of every arising visual problem and countering unseen problems.

Success has a very intricate beginning, an overall convoluted business process and a moving end-targeted goal. The art to achieving success has to start with a well-defined structure. The structure should be built with an interlinking, collaborated partnering business process that we call **"OBT Strategic Teaming™."** The OBT Strategic Teaming process is developed with many types of innovative interconnecting resources. We explain our process as analogous to a tree or a building. In order for a tree to grow or the building to stand tall, to attain success you have to have many sub-processes to fulfill the overall process.

Our process covers more than what I can explain in the book, but I will highlight some of the intricate parts covering the attainment of success:

- At the beginning, you have to logically figure out the proper place (marketplace) to start your structure making certain the ground for the structure can be supported with maximum strength. *(A place in the ground where the soil is fertile for tree growth to develop a well-defined rooting system.)*
- As you construct the structural support in the ground, you place interlinking piers and reinforcement to make certain the beams stand strong in the ground to provide a very strong foundation. *(This would the stage in business where you would create relationships that extend trust, resources and valuable similar goals for success.)*
- In your preparation for upward growth, you have to expand your relationships in alignment with various strategic paths so that your growth develops innovative extensions of resources at every aligned portion of your business model. *(This would be illustrated similarly to a tree trunk that grows upward and the branches grow outward from the trunk providing bearing fruit and leaves.)*
- Importantly, to maintain a successful growth of business, you have to nurture the interconnecting relationships between teaming partners, business development partners, potential clients, clients, government agencies and other resource supporters. *(This would be illustrated like watering the roots of a tree.)*

As you build your overall "Sustainment Model for Success **(SMS),**" you have to construct a stronghold business process with adaptability, determination, durability, flexibility, persistency and tenacity. You should equip yourself with knowledgeable people based on your business process. You should maintain all information about your business in a completely confidential manner. Always protect your success by all measures of defense. The more success you attain, the more untrustworthy people will attempt to attach themselves to you and your business. Beware of these people because they are not looking to share business growth in a collaborated relationship form.

Setting the Tone

Logically, you should position your entire business to be invisible to your client base except for marketing and branding during your initial stages of development. Don't expose yourself to the marketplace until you are ready to precisely perform business. Perform extensive research *(i.e. do your homework)*, scour case studies and strategically carry out your due diligence. Gather vital information on how other entrepreneurs/small business owners have accomplished success for their businesses, but also learn of their failures.

Once you have created your business structure, formed enduring relationships at all levels, located a strategic position in the government marketplace and developed an innovative means to indirectly meet your potential clients, make certain you are highly prepared prior to the first direct meeting conversation with the potential client. Your first impression will be a lasting impression according to your potential client.

Cultivate and nurture your client relationship by several innovative ways that will impact your ability to create a stronger and more trustworthy relationship:

- Meet with your clients in informal settings when possible such as:
  - Lunch
  - Dinner
  - Golfing events
  - Other casual, relaxed places where you can create a more personal discussion without interruption, but choose an environment that has a neutral setting.
- Schedule meetings (both informal and formal) to discuss goal settings for both parties mutually, but direct the discussion initially on what can benefit them first and foremost.
- Discuss topics with them that have a positive spin of their business progression. Prior to your meeting, you should research an impressive accomplishment through their efforts.
- Always focus everything mutually between both parties and always try to stay current about marketplace industry changes that may impact your client's business positively or negatively.
- Generally, when time permits, provide an opportunity for your client to collaboratively participate in future events.

It is very important to ensure that your small business is aligned with strategic inner and outer innovative resources. Make certain that you construct your team to be composed of a variety of strategically aligned expertise and certified entities in Government Contracting as follows to create not only a competitive advantage, but to achieve a multi-functional advantage:

* **Small Business** *(Advantage: Two or more strategic small businesses with the right mixture of experience and expertise combine to develop a great arsenal of services.)*

* **VOSB**—**Veteran Owned Small Business** *(Advantage: A VOSB may not have contracts set-asides, but the network alone entails a great benefit.)*

* **SDVOSB**—**Service Disabled Veteran Owned Small Business** *(Advantage: Executive Order 13360 directs that at least 3 percent of all federal agencies' contracting dollars go to businesses owned by service-disabled veterans. The good news is that agencies are actively seeking service-disabled, veteran-owned small businesses as vendors.)*

* **WOSB/EDWOSB**—**Woman Owned Small Business/ Economically Disadvantaged Woman Owned Small Business** *(Advantage: There is a 3 percent requirement for all federal agencies' contracting dollars to go to businesses owned by 51 percent woman-owned businesses. It is important to understand that the business has to be certified. The (4) Third Party SBA WOSB Certifiers: 1.) El Paso Hispanic Chamber of Commerce; 2.) National Women Business Owners Corporation; 3.) US Women's Chamber of Commerce; 4.) Women's Business Enterprise National Council (WBENC.))*

* **HUB Zone** **(Historically Underutilized Business) Small Business** (Advantage: There are **2 levels of Federal**

benefits: (1.) relates directly to Federal contracts. There are 4 types of HUB Zone contract opportunities: *a.) Competitive, b.) Sole Source, c.) Full and Open, d.) Subcontracting and* (2.) involves specialized assistance: *a.) Eligible HUB Zone firms can qualify for higher SBA-guaranteed surety bonds on construction and service contract bids, b.) Firms in Federal Empowerment Zones and Enterprise Communities (EZ/EC) can also benefit from employer tax credits, tax-free facility bonds and investment tax deductions.*)

- **8a Business Development Program** (U.S. Small Business Administration) *(Advantage: Small businesses that are considered to be socially and economically disadvantaged can receive assistance under SBA's nine-year 8(a) Business Development Program. SBA helps these firms develop and grow their businesses through one-to-one counseling, training workshops and management and technical guidance. It also provides access to government contracting opportunities, allowing them to become solid competitors in the federal marketplace.)*

- **Large Company** *(Advantage: There are no set-asides for large companies, but they have proven long-term relationships and contracts. They have a lot more resources which provide them much greater abilities to break the barriers in Federal contracting.)*

- **Universities** *(Advantage: There are flow-down subcontracting opportunities and R&D Grant opportunities. There are huge benefits for educational institutions in Federal contracting.)*

- **Non-Profit Organizations** *(Advantage: Eligible for certain programs including Federal & State grants, financial assistance, Government surplus and tax exemptions.)*

By combining expertise and skills with some of the entities above, this will create an extreme strategic advantage that will separate you from your competitors. Remember when setting your foundation, you have to develop an innovative resource business model. You should ensure every step of your business is strategically aligned while never assuming anything. Always validate every business decision you make and implement early in your business process two important characteristics: *Checking System of Validation (CSV) and a Business & Personal Protection System (BPPS.)*

Getting through the Adversity, Obstacles and Struggles

ADVERSITY

This is subject matter that we all will face one day. This is also an area that I know all too well. Understand and know the limitations of these particular words, their meanings and strongly know there power of action. While it is important for you to know your business, it is critical to know the downfalls of your business more fully and with much more agility and definition.

Let's define the terms below. While these words may seem general, believe me, they are a harsh set of "words of power and adverse action."

What do the terms Adverse, Adversity, Obstacles, Struggles, Strife and Strive mean?

Adverse: Acting against or in a contrary direction; unfavorable.
Adversity: Hard times, misfortune.
Obstacles: Something that stands in the way or opposes.
Struggles: To make strenuous efforts against opposition. Strive. To proceed with difficulty or with great efforts. Contest, Strife
Strife: Conflict, fight, struggle.
Strive: To make effort, hard labor. To struggle in opposition, contend, endeavor, attempt, and try.

Most statistical data reference business failures by adverse conditions which normally result in adversity. Often times there are huge roadblocks in the way of an Entrepreneur's path.

Many times it is not just the roadblocks that stand in the way, but the opposition that comes in many different forms:

- Savvy business professionals with bad intentions pertaining to your business or you.
- Business Professionals whom we call "Takers" that have no intentions to give anything to you but "hardship."
- The so-called professionals that are the most persuasive whom we call "Talkers." This type of person is the loudest talker in the room, in the building. They want to be your friend something bad. They will initially try to do anything for you before you even ask. They are very aggressive, overwhelming, outspoken and must talk over everyone to make up for the knowledge that they don't possess in the

first place. Stay a considerable distance away from these type of people. They will literally kick you if you come close to a downward spiral in business. They will try to absorb as much information from you as possible. *(A word of advice: Don't let them in your circle of trust. This will be discussed in Chapter 9 in further details.)* In other words, if you leave your business ideas exposed, they will try to take possession of them.

• These individuals call themselves "Friends." Notice that I said they call themselves friends. We all know that "True Friends" are hard to come by. True friends are by your side no matter what you may go through and will always hold your best interest to heart. Neither money nor materialistic items can divide your relationship. They will not believe negative comments about you without first reaching out to you. They will always be supportive of you even if they do not understand or fully support what you are doing in business.

• Last, but not least, is what we call our "Friends" because we have mutually grown a secure bond with each other. The test of friendship that is always a reliable test of depth of friendship is the dissension of money. A lot of times money can be a true blessing, but when rapid success comes and a great deal of potential profit maybe on the horizon, you will see if true friendship will stand the test of time.

• Adversity usually comes unexpectedly and swiftly. This is why it is extremely important to prepare yourself with the greatest business foundation, structure, process and methodology that you can possibly create. Do not cut corners, accept satisfaction and always prepare with excellence.

Naturally, we can't prepare for every unknown situation, but we can prepare for the known situations that have occurred to many other Entrepreneurs.

After experiencing adversity, I have learned a great deal of realistic life-changing measures and countermeasures to not only deal with adversity when face-to-face with it, but innovative ways to prevent the adversity in the first place. I truly know that I can be a great asset to other Entrepreneurs because I have lived the reality of the defined example of adversity. Before I provide the measures and countermeasures to help you in your entrepreneurial journey, I want to go a little further in discussing what extends from adversity known as **"Obstacles and Struggles."** I want to provide some innovative means of building against adversity, obstacles and struggles with some strategic business process tools in reference to **"Strife and Strive."**

OBSTACLES

An area of blockage known as "Obstacles" in your business cycle comes in many forms. Obstacles can be definite causes of business failure. However, you can overcome the impact of obstacles if you decide not to give up on your dreams. Statistically, many Entrepreneurs never recover from certain obstacles that come in their business path directly or indirectly. A reason for this is because they do not provide "Contingency Planning" which is very important in the longevity of their business. If an Entrepreneur happens to have a contingency plan, you can almost guarantee that they will never plan for the most devastating obstacles and rarely plan for run-of-the-mill obstacles. *"The situation normally presents itself in a way that the Entrepreneur would never think that it would happen to him or her so they don't provide the depth of the contingency plan to counter the worst condition."*

It is very difficult when an obstacle of any kind occurs, but you have to prepare yourself to expect the worst. Never assume that an obstacle has only one part or that it is a short-term occurrence. As a matter of fact, a lot of obstacles that can arise may take years to overcome. What is your level of endurance? How much are you willing to give? What is your limit of tolerance? What is your breaking point or do you even have one?

<u>I will provide you with some strong, real-life advice to think about when you are placed in a situation of an overwhelming obstacle:</u>

- Your level of endurance should be higher than you can possibly imagine. You should not have a maximum level because your mindset should be to withstand any kind of obstacle, no matter how extreme it may appear.
- At the birth of your business, you should've made a commitment to get to your measure of success no matter what. Your commitment should be structured to withstand any amount of disruption.
- Prior to starting your business, you should have adopted an unlimited point of tolerance to deal with any business obstacle, if not, adopt one now!
- You should not have a breaking point because no obstacle should be able to disrupt your dreams.
- Never let anyone create so much opposition towards you or your business that it derails your direction to success.
- Stay focused on your path to success no matter how many people try to drive your focus to its demise.

- Stay on the journey to success no matter what others may say negatively towards what you are doing.
- When you are dealing with obstacles, never let anyone know the opposition that you are struggling with.
- Don't trust just anyone, trust those that have earned your trust, or they will be your obstacle.

Here are a few more obstacles listed below:

- Certain individuals that don't want you to be successful
- Competitors
- Lack of due diligence
- Lack of funding
- Lack of knowledge
- No business plan or poorly defined plan
- No business structure
- Self
- Unknowledgeable Contracting personnel
- Unknowledgeable Human Resources personnel
- Wrong targeted industry area or client

STRUGGLES

Entrepreneurs will have their share of having to overcome many forms of opposition. You have to really create momentum and an extreme mode of motivation to get through these struggles of your business journey. I am not trying to set a negative or harsh tone about business, I just want you to be ready for the realities of your entrepreneurial journey.

People always discuss success, failures, difficulties but fail to mention "Struggles." The only resolution to overcome adversity and obstacles will be the ability to strive through the struggle or strife.

Struggles need to be overcome in confidential settings. Keep them in the background if possible. No one needs to know that you are struggling. Exceptions would be individuals that may be of great help to you, especially your support structure of business (i.e. Spouse, Children, Friends and/or trusted individuals of your choice.)

Your efforts to overcome struggles can be achieved in many forms.

I will list a few strong-proven efforts that I have implemented as well as other successful entrepreneurs:

- Keep your faith when fighting through the struggle.
- Maintain all pertinent business documents, including the envelopes that stored the documents. There is great value in the envelopes because most will carry a date to validate a postmark date. If it is a shipping package slip, it will carry important information about the sender, receiver, date, address, contact numbers and who signed for the package. This can be of crucial importance.
- Keep detailed records (payroll, human resource materials, job applications, phone records, receipts and all other documents even if they seem insignificant.) File these items in a safe place, preferably in a remote location separate from your office.

- Stay strong and never show the stress and anxiety in your facial expressions.
- Never assume anything that may carry a legal consequence. Always validate everything.
- When handling financial and legal business with employees of any capacity, always make certain that there are three or more employees involved.
- Always maintain your business professionally and never mix with personal situations. Keep them separated at all times.

Surviving adversity generates strength and either a willingness to succeed or an acceptance of complete failure. Always strive to achieve unlimited strategies to build your toolbox of business defenses for various types of struggles. You have to build your business arsenal just the same as our military continues to build for perfection.

When developing and planning for the unexpected struggles that may come your way, make certain that you plan for the following areas:

- Your position in the industry marketplace for the country's economy both presently and in the future.
- Political status as it may impact your industry marketplace.
- Identify your business resources that may apply to your industry to bring benefits to your business
- Identify sources as quickly as possible that will be trusted resources for your business (i.e. business associates, friends, family, investors, legal, etc.)

Remember "success" attracts great resources that you are able to harness for your business strategy. But remember success also brings unwanted and damaging resources.

Measures	Countermeasures
Due Diligence at Multi-Levels	Build Protection Strategies from the Due Diligence
Detailed Check & Balance	Build a Financial, Legal & Security interlinking system of protection
There are many more measures and countermeasures that you should create to provide a well-diverse and balanced protection system to avoid the overwhelming impact of Adversity, Obstacles and Struggles!	

How to connect the dots to do Government Business—THE UNTOLD STORY!

Entrepreneurs and Small Business Owners can be successful in the Federal Government contracting industry by producing substantial profits and long-term business stability. In order for success to be accomplished, there must be a sequential order of function. Statistically, over the years, especially in today's economy, there has been a very high percentage of small businesses that proceed into the unfavorable waters of "Business Closure" and "Failure."

History has shown that the Federal Government contracting industry is very complex and extremely difficult to penetrate by way of small businesses. What should get your attention is the entity that doesn't have such a complex and difficult journey to success in Government contracting is "Large Businesses." Most small businesses are under the impression that large businesses do well because they have a substantial amount of funds, resources and influence in the industry. Well, you are partially correct. However, most large businesses do well by many other reasons.

I will connect you with a few concepts that will add great value to hopefully get you to the next level of success:

- Advanced Innovative Intelligence **(AII)**
- Credibility for Branding and Marketing **(CBM)**
- Credibility for Marketplace Penetration **(CMP)**
- Geographical Selective Positioning **(GSP)**

Here are a few concepts that I recommend from experience that we have used in our innovative strategic solutions toolbox:

- Generational Concept Connection **(GCC)**
- Precise Penetration Positioning **(3Ps or PPP)**
- Strategic Impact Relationships **(SIR)**

Our solutions are successfully proven by many levels of experience from our strategic teaming relationships with large businesses. From a National to Global standpoint, we have conceptually developed a special process of innovative relationships known as "OBT Teaming™" or "OBT Strategic Teaming™".

Let's talk about "how to connect dots to do Government business." The most important contributing factor of an unlinked process of Government is truly the untold story of how everything interlinks to achieve success in the Federal Marketplace. I am sure that there are at least a few ways to successfully understand the connection, the process of this complex market. After spending a couple of decades in the Federal Marketplace, working within the support structure, collaborating military interlinking, combining private& public sector support and consulting for the market, a connection of success in the industry becomes clear. But this only happened after quite amount of time of understanding the marketplace.

Here are a few things to keep in mind that you should implement in your initial process of planning:

- Take the time to understand the history of the Federal Marketplace.
- Do your due diligence to truly understand the total marketplace structure.
- Gain understanding of where or if your services or products fit in the marketplace.
- Ensure that your services or products is a great benefit to the Federal Government, we call it "Niche for Necessity **(NFN.)**"
- Once you have achieved a "Receipt of Understanding (ROU)" about your services or products, then the real work begins. You are about start this long business journey.
- Build your strategic structure which we call the "OBT Strategic Structure™," This is composed of a lot of areas and sub areas. We mention many of these areas in this book. We have an **Entrepreneurial Book Series (EBS)—called "Operation Breakthrough: Entrepreneurial Paths to Success™ (EPS)"** coming to the market soon that will breakdown the total process that can be used in a self-pace manner, as well as in the form of "Strategic Educational Instruction™ (SEI.)"

- Teaming by Credibility™ (TBC) is a strategic process of Operation Breakthrough Strategies. There are many innovative and strategic levels of processes and methodologies that I can't cover entirely in this book alone, but I will highlight effectively some of the areas that will hopefully help many entrepreneurs and small business owners throughout this book.

This should be executed prior to conducting external business in the Federal Marketplace. I know that there are a lot of you that wish you knew this prior to already having spent years of attempting to do business in the Federal Government market. I won't tell you to stop where you are in your process of business pursuit, but I will tell you to definitely engage these ideas immediately to avoid continuous misdirected paths to success.

THE UNTOLD STORY

In the Federal Government Marketplace of contracting, it is known to be like a maze, a misguided road with no signage for directions, a roller coaster ride that has no end or a path with no connections to get you to your end point. It is basically seen as a bureaucracy with no content which illustrates a process or pattern made up of a vicious business cycle that has no connecting points to form a cycle.

It is always a great enigma for Entrepreneurs, Small Business Owners, Business Development professionals and associated professionals to even develop a process to get them in a direct path of understanding Government contacting.

The conferences, seminars, symposiums, breakout sessions and other events that take place in the Federal Government Marketplace do not provide connecting processes, but they provide lots of informational materials that have unlinked business procedures. In Chapter 7, I will discuss more information about how to gain value through conferences, seminars, symposiums, breakout sessions and other events.

Entrepreneurs and Small Business Owners, by nature of their business marketplace, whether public or private sector, always work in a one-track tunnel. This happens because they are rightfully trying to protect their business interests. Well, this is something that needs to change strategically so that there are countermeasures established by way of multi-level support. The multi-level support system broadens your ability to overcome adversity, obstacles and struggles. Based on my experience, which I recommend to all Entrepreneurs and Business Owners, is that they should implement a support system at the beginning stages of business.

Remember when you are going through an adverse situation, always stay positive, stay close to people you trust and distance yourself from untrustworthy people. Generally, during times of adversity, you will be overwhelmed by all types of negative barriers that will occupy your time. While in this moment, it will seem like each day is never-ending, each week is dreadful and the months are interminable. Cling to your faith, stay strong internally and maintain your external image as if you had the greatest day ever. But you should maintain your mindset that no matter what you have to go through, nothing will stop your pathway to success. You may be delayed, obstructed, disrupted, frustrated and totally overpowered, but continue to strive with great tenacity, agility, faith and self-motivation.

PART IV

CONCEPT TO COMPLEXITY!

INNOVATION—TEAMING BY CREDIBILITY!

Chapter 4

The Concept to Credibility to Conclusion for launch of the business journey!

Value of Determination

The effort I put into achieving any given task is above the average person's threshold. While others may flounder when the odds are totally stacked against them to achieve a driven task, for me, my mind is at complete ease to face the challenge head-on. During my career, I always plotted to accomplish more than my colleagues. I would seek to make certain I accomplished two, frequently four or more tasks when everyone else was concentrating on one single point of interest. I truly think that it takes a great level of risk-taking when setting to be a truly determined individual. The greater the determination, the greater chance of failure which creates a limited amount of entrepreneurs who achieve success.

As an entrepreneur, my level of determination has no fail option. I truly have taken failure out of my tools of determination. In one's self-drive to ultimately build one's self with an abundance of "determination," one must equip him or herself with many internal driving measures as follows:

1. *Define your measure of success.*
2. *Set your goals.*
3. *Primary Keys to Effective Goal Setting*
4. *Set your expectations high.*
5. *Understand your capabilities and abilities.*
6. *Keep your strengths in the forefront and continue to develop your weaknesses.*
7. *Develop strategies to develop your goals.*
8. *Utilize technology as an empowering tool.*
9. *Work hard, but smart, persevere and remain flexible and adaptable.*
10. *Work from a support structure of relevance to align your goals.*
11. *Develop and associate yourself with a support network of individuals that will enhance your capabilities and abilities.*
12. *Gather all resources needed to accomplish what you set out to do.*

(1) Define your measure of success:

In order for you to maximize your ability to achieve the proper measure of determination, you have to set parameters and markers at the limits to what you want for success. Never set your goals by someone else's standards. Always be precise on what your goals are in order to meet your level of success. Many entrepreneurs measure their success by what personal goals they are trying to meet for their business. I measure my success by several ways and implement check points along the way such as follows:

a. *Meeting goals and expectations that I originally set*
b. *Monetary amounts that I set based on contracts achieved*
c. *Revenue amounts*
d. *Other individuals I have helped to achieved their goals*
e. *Recognitions earned*
f. *The request of others for my assistance to help them with their goals to achieve success*

In your pursuit of success, always clarify all degrees of what you are trying accomplish. Learn from each and every step and any struggles you had along the way and log them so that you can easily get to your next goal without repeating any mistakes made prior. This will truly reduce the time spent on your journey toward success.

- *The Measure of Success is not how you are challenged; it is how you respond to the challenge!*
- *The Measure of Success is not how you succeed, but how you react and respond from failure!*

- *The Measure of Success is not how you receive success, but how you carry out daily practice after you achieve success!*
- *The Measure of Success is how you rebound from losing Family members and Friends through unexpected occurrences from business!*
- *The Measure of Success is how you cope with adversity to achieve success!*
- *The Measure of Success is how failure comes into your life during your journey of business success and you maintain your faith in God, continuously and consistently!*
- *The Measure of Success is how you believe over a shadow of a doubt even when people around you change for the worst!*

SUCCESS = Strategy + Innovation + Planning + Execution = **TEAMING**

SUCCESS = Success under Continuous Committed Entrepreneurial Strategic Structure

(2) Set your goals

Most statistics and research specifies when entrepreneurs set measurable goals for themselves and their companies, they normally will greatly achieve them. For example, when I engage in my goal setting, I define my objectives in a pragmatic form which provides me with measurable terms. In my opinion, Entrepreneurs need to be great project and program managers or expedite the capabilities so that they can identify their resources, costs and needed funds they will need in order to invest in their companies. I developed an "action plan" that I will define in great detail as to where I wanted my company to go, then developed an implementation plan followed by an execution plan. Once you know what your goals are and where you want to go in accomplishing your goals, the next important step is to figure out how you'll get there and how much you're willing to spend on your journey.

Setting your goals can be a challenging situation at many levels. Once you set your goals, never leverage for smaller adjustments to these goals for less to achieve your goals quicker. This will diminish your ultimate goal and result in less revenue, lack of motivation and an overall potential of eliminating your business' success. When setting goals, always set achievable limits and always monitor the entire process throughout. When obstacles and roadblocks arise, immediately take them head-on. Be aggressive, yet strategic when attacking the obstacles and roadblocks. Get a full understanding of what the problem may be and develop a plan of action to eliminate or resolve the problem.

Prior to setting any of your goals as an Entrepreneur, build a large variety of resources that you have researched from other entrepreneurs, so that you can eliminate repetitive problems. Resource-building before launching your business should be one of your main goals because this will create a source for any entrepreneur to be able to relate to any obstacle or roadblock. In your resource-building, each entrepreneur should study their market industry, business sector and sort out resources composed of people with capabilities to support you in your goal setting. You should be able to access informational materials that provide a great host of supporting data, technological internet resources and an associated consortium of teaming partners that add great value to your company. Keep in mind that you need to be able to add value to their company as well in forming your consortium of teaming partners. Once you develop your combined host of resources, define them by easily, accessible categories and solution areas so that you can retrieve solutions very quickly. Responding to any obstacle quickly can reduce cost, eliminate duration of obstacle and ultimately achieve your path to accomplishing your goal.

In your journey of achieving your goals, always lay out a well-structured plan of action. Always break down your goal into several parts so that you can define the *how, what, where, why and when* in order to successfully accomplish your goal. This makes matters much easier when you are trying to accomplish your goal.

In your goal setting process, always ensure that you "pay close attention to detail" to make certain that you completely reach every aspect of the goal. Setting and achieving goals is where success happens! We often get stuck at the beginning or the middle of the "goal" process with assessing our situation and setting goals without following through to completion. Setting goals without achieving them in my business mind calculates to failure.

I define failure as simply missing the mark, not achieving my essential mission. As an entrepreneur, if you don't set any goals for yourself, you could say you have succeeded because you didn't fail. But by this logic, you never achieve any success to measure your company. Setting and achieving goals is the mainstay of business success. The successful entrepreneur mindset uses goal-directed logic in every aspect of designing, implementing and execution of a business.

Effective goal setting occurs when we choose goals that we believe we can truly achieve. We keep those goals ever in front of us, never losing sight of where we want to go in life as an entrepreneur. The groundwork for effective goal setting starts with these crucial components.

(3)   **Primary Keys to Effective Goal Setting**

Key #1—Originate with a fully detailed vision for yourself and your business. Without a visual image of how your business will look in the future, you will not be able to set all of your daily, weekly and monthly goals that will propel your business beyond your imagination into reality.

Key #2—Know your passions that drive your goals—Often the problem with goals isn't in setting them; however, it is being motivated to actually achieve the goals you've set up. Think about what really gets you fired up about your goals initially and maintain that passion and you will reach your goals. Always keep in the forefront of your mind what drives your dreams and achieving your goals will follow. Your passions need to be behind your list of goals and fuel the fire that makes you respond until the completion of the goal. Goal setting without action is what? Simply put, a diversion, an obstacle, a roadblock, a failure of just merely stating what you could possibly accomplish, but never achieve.

Key #3—Be brutally honest with yourself—Setting goals means being honest with yourself and others to accomplish a dedicated mission. Achieving your goal requires complete honesty. Always look deep inside yourself to ensure certainty; know your strengths and weaknesses. Don't pretend to have skills, capabilities or talents that simply don't exist within you; however, strive to strengthen where you are weak. It is a major waste of your time and energy to strive to be someone else when being yourself requires no additional work. Always be the most motivated at your lowest points and your stride to achieving your goals will come easier and be measured at a shorter distance of accomplishment.

Key #4—Set your own goals in order to achieve—Commit to setting your goals, not what you have seen others accomplish. Your only way of achieving "Your Goals" is to accept no failure. For you to achieve the goals you have set before you, you must have strong faith within yourself that the goals you are working toward will take your life and business in the direction you want to go. Don't take on goals for yourself that were designed by someone else because it will take you down a path of wasted time and take you further away from your dreams. Look at your life, cling to your God-given faith and your vision will guide you toward your goals.

Key #5—Live a Life of Action—Lots of Entrepreneurs run their business off their goals, but never achieve them because they apply no action and they settle for less than their goal. Spend your time wisely and don't compromise your drive to accomplish your goal. Remember to spend less time on setting your goals than executing them. If you have a tendency to get stuck in the "planning" stage of goal setting, then start with setting smaller, achievable goals each day that you make a priority to reach before the end of each day.

(4) Set your Expectations High

Many times throughout my career, I have witnessed fellow entrepreneurs set their expectations for either their company or self-driven goals too high or too low. Most often, entrepreneurs tend to set their expectations in a manageable reach of success, but most don't link their expectations with their business plan, their ability to achieve success in teaming relationships and they do not align their expectations with alternative support to these expectations that are set at such a high level. For those entrepreneurs that set their expectations high and meet their goals, they often achieve them because they set markers to boost each level of expectation to the ultimate peak of success.

Still, there are an alarming number of measures that an entrepreneur can take to save lots of money, time and effort by maximizing their resources that are normally in their reach such as:

1. Always gather information and execute from what you have witnessed from other entrepreneurs that do things exemplary. Most often, entrepreneurs tend to see more opportunities creatively than the average person, but most do not act on them. That is one of the things that set apart most entrepreneurs. Entrepreneurs that take big risks usually act immediately without hesitancy. This is great when measures of success for high expectations are set, which makes the overall result astonishing.

2. Set both yourself and your business up with a business resource platform that will always bring added resources to you every step of the way. These platforms are normally

presented in a national setting. But be very careful on the platform you choose and make sure it is aligned with your expectations.

3. As an entrepreneur, get creative and innovative in your expectations by supporting them with previous case studies, experiences from others, failures of other entrepreneurs, limitations of what you can achieve. No entrepreneur achieves high expectations alone. The best of us have many resource tools, people, organizations and the ability to communicate very well in achieving our expectations in a plan of action.

In the 2005, first global study of high-expectation entrepreneurship, it found that just 9.8% of the world's entrepreneurs were expected to create almost 75% of the jobs generated by new business ventures. **High-expectation entrepreneurship** in start-ups and newly formed businesses, which expect to employ at least 20 employees within five years, often fail if they do not form a resource of teaming. These ventures have far-reaching consequences for the economies in which they operate, particularly because of their impact on job creation and innovation when they utilize their resources and team with others.

High-expectation entrepreneurial activity occurs in North America (USA and Canada) more than any other country in a recent study. The ability for each entrepreneur to achieve his or her expectations are unlimited if he or she utilizes his or her resources wisely. Worldwide, 9.8% of entrepreneurs expect to create 74.1% of all jobs born out of new business ventures.

In 2009, that same 9.8% of the world's entrepreneur, which is significantly more entrepreneurs, the expectancy of jobs creation is about 92%. This impacts our national-to-global economy greatly. This is why it is important for me to help as many entrepreneurs as possible so that our economy can grow and meet its expectations at the highest possible level.

While I will add a few tidbits of advice toward your setting your high expectations, always include this short list, even though it is not all inclusive:

1. Understand your clarity of leadership (i.e. Executives, Managers, Consultants, administrative) at all levels.
2. Be creative in your openness to discuss logic with other entrepreneurs, but also be strategic to not diminish your expectations at a high level by receiving negative feedback from others because they may not understand your expectations and may pass on unreliable information that may cause your expectations to fail.
3. Make certain your organizational capabilities provides the support and resources to sustain your high expectations.
4. Make certain you maintain the flexibility to change while striving to reach your high expectations, but maintain directional vision and stay the path of your expectation.
5. Maximize your capacity to think for one's self by achieving impressive abilities of discovery.

Overcome obstacles and failures and maintain tenacity and determination to succeed no matter the odds. As Psalm 23 states: *Yea, though I walk through the valley of the shadow of death, I will fear no evil.*

(5)   Understand your Capabilities and Abilities

As an entrepreneur, you have to initially measure every ability and capability you possess. You have to be very critical on yourself as to what your true limitations are and what resources you have readily available for yourself. You have to continuously measure yourself daily to make certain you understand your capabilities, minimum and maximum abilities. Even if you feel that you have a lot of abilities, always seek more so that you continue to grow.

There are many important factors that make up what your capabilities and abilities consist of so that you fully understand how you can maximize them:

- Understanding your attitude towards risk and reward is essential for a happy life as an entrepreneur.
- If you have most of the aforementioned characteristics of motivation and drive, then you will be better equipped.
- When you analyze yourself, stay away from lofty estimations of your abilities.
- Be candid about your personality and capabilities.
- If you lack certain abilities and capabilities, it's better to know that. Understanding that before moving forward into a prolonged venture that will consume your time and money and can also cause failure will save you a major headache.
- Many mistakes and emotional scars can be averted if you understand your limitations and move to correct them before getting in too deep.
- Hopefully as an entrepreneur, you built your capabilities and abilities throughout your entire career, this is one of the things I did to maximize my abilities and capabilities.

- Hopefully as an entrepreneur, you performed either a self-test or some type of testing to measure your abilities and capabilities.

- Make certain to surround yourself or to associate with other professionals and entrepreneurs that can elevate your capabilities and expand your abilities.

- Make certain you gather continuous feedback from others that can help you measure, build and increase your capabilities through detailed structure.

- Make certain when you seek to build your capabilities and abilities from other entrepreneurs, you get every aspect of understanding so that you will grow effectively.

- Make certain to obtain various forms of mentorship from other entrepreneurs, professionals in targeted areas of your business, seniors to you that have obtained a great amount of experience. If in government business, seek experienced officials with knowledge you would like to obtain and build a team of professionals, an advisory board or at least a resource pool of professionals that you can reach out to for fast solutions.

As an entrepreneur, your capabilities stem from your career. Always input your capabilities into your business plan in the greatest of detail. Your personal capabilities will most likely extend great value to your business capabilities. Make certain your abilities are utilized to enhance your business process.

(6)   Keep your strengths in the forefront and continue to develop your weaknesses

My opinion of being an effective entrepreneur means you have to place your strengths in the forefront of doing business. When you interact with many others to conduct business, people tend to challenge you in every aspect. You have to always be ready and up for the challenge. As an entrepreneur with higher levels of success, comes higher levels of challenges. You have to always stay innovative in your thinking and execute your strengths in multiple levels across-the-board to face your challengers.

While continuing your entrepreneurial journey, always continue to strengthen your weaknesses in the background. Often entrepreneurs place themselves in a comprising position because they expose their weaknesses too many times in the forefront while conducting business. For example, when a small business presents its weakness to a large business while conducting contract work, the large company will focus on the weakness. In turn, they will tend to treat you based on your weaknesses, not your strengths. One exposed weakness outdoes 10 to 15 strengths and it takes a lot of effort to remove that weakness out of the forefront. However, if you should somehow expose this weakness, it is not the end of your business journey. You have to use some innovative methods to exploit your strengths in a magnified way of overpowering your weakness that was exposed. Importantly, you want ensure that you have identified the weakness, corrected it and make certain your client knows and understands how you corrected it, but not draw large attention to the matter.

Concentrate on taking maximum advantage of your strengths. If you're the only source available for a particular product or solution, you have tremendous leverage across the board. If economic conditions have created a market in which the product you're selling is in great demand coupled with a low supply, it gives you more bargaining power to name your price. If you are the buyer in a depressed economy, you normally have the advantage of too much supply and lower demand. The current housing situation is a classic example of what happens when supply vastly outweighs the demand and market prices fall dramatically.

When developing your weaknesses to strengths, always gather vast amounts of information to sustain your situation. Log every step in accomplishing your mission and never move to the next step until you fully understand what you have accomplished. Even if you seek outside assistance to help you in transitioning your weakness to strengths, always make certain you fully understand the process.

A lot of times, entrepreneurs have a tendency to move diligently to get to the next step, but you must understand what people are doing for you in any process that helps you so that you do not form a dependency of need in your future processes. Meaning, if someone helps you with a problem and you do not understand what was defined in the solution, then when you come across another problem, you will more than likely stand still until someone comes and solves the process for you. This causes you to miss or delay your goals and ultimately, takes you off of your path to success. Sometimes you have to outsource certain things, but make certain whatever you outsource, you fully understand the process involved to gain greater understanding.

(7)   Develop Strategies to Develop your Goals

Entrepreneurs are innovative and creative in development in all areas. As an entrepreneur, you have to innovatively develop strategies in various forms and stages. From what I have experienced and from what I have heard from most other entrepreneurs is that you have to go back to the basics, the beginning, an initial core of business process.

1. The beginning: In order to create a strategy, you will need to analyze from where you have started. Write down the history of your business, the purpose of the organization, the mission and the business model that you follow. Along with this, determine what the strengths of your business are in ranking order.

2. Define your goals. The next step to analyzing your business and yourself is to define your goals. This will include "objects of desire," meaning what you want to achieve and what you visualize for your business for the next year, two years and even ten years. You should include a vision and objectives to this section.

3. Start building your strategy. This is the point where you define how you will achieve the goals and mission of your business. You should include things such as: customers you want, how you will get the customers, what plans and projects aren't working with the company and what steps should be taken instead.

4. Admit your weaknesses. One of the most overlooked parts of businesses is identifying your weaknesses and entrepreneurs will often times fail to reach their goals

because of this. You will want to define what these are and figure out ways to overcome them. This can include things such as: what is the limit of my capabilities, what are my maximum abilities, what capabilities do my management teams possess, what are their abilities, what resources do I have on-hand to support my development of goals and a measuring device to measure my goals to completion.

5. Build steps to overcome the weaknesses. You will want to focus on specific tactics and plans to overcome your obstacles. This includes competitive advantages, as well as how you will reach the forces that are causing weaknesses. Combine this with the strategy that you have already built and you will have a plan for success.

My experience in developing my strategies and goals has been an easier process because as I built my Teaming Partner relationships, my Advisory Board of experts, organizations and associations I affiliated myself with accompanied my quest. I wholeheartedly created an innovative resource bank of solutions that created pre-scenarios to setting my goals, examples of successful achievements to goals, solutions to problems that allowed me to mold a goal with huge support at all levels. My recommendation as an entrepreneur is to strategically build all of the relationships that surround your entire business, your goals, your success and you will gain great results.

(8)   Utilize technology as an empowering tool

In today's times, technology is a powerful, empowering tool that entrepreneurs need to embrace more to enhance their business in more ways than recognized. Technology changes by the day and the more entrepreneurs and their staffs stay abreast of the many types of technology to help their business, the more efficient and faster they can accomplish various tasks.

Entrepreneurs need to understand the maximum benefit that technology can produce in their everyday efforts. My opinion is that every entrepreneur needs to remain aware of various types of technology that support our daily business actions.

From the basics of Laptops and Desktops, an entrepreneur can have themselves well-equipped and ahead of the curve of advanced capabilities as it pertains to technology that will cut their administrative costs by 90%, reduce their needed staff by 20%. But technology can help a staff become more diversified and multi-functional to produce an increase in work performance output.

As the entrepreneur, there are many different types of software that provide a source of unlimited tools to implement almost any task needed for your business. The different types of software range from desktop publishing, business and productivity, digital publishing, training, utilities, web publishing, database, financial, multimedia, OCR, presentation, organization, project management, spreadsheets, word processing, engineering & CAD, GIS Mapping, technical writing, language and many other applications.

In these times, communication can occur globally through a click of a button. Entrepreneurs can host meetings throughout the country from technology to communicate functionally across the country and even globally. From a mobile standpoint, through technology, entrepreneurs are able to conduct business throughout the nation at any given geographical location. This saves money, time and man-hour cost for the entire company's bottom line.

Through the use of websites, companies can market anywhere in the world with minimal expenses. This saves a tremendous amount of marketing costs. You are able to communicate with anyone worldwide and even provide real-time communications.

Emailing is essential in today's technological times to provide a communication resource for a small business owner, entrepreneur, professional, administrative person, basically everyone in an organization to communicate globally. This source of communication also allows people within your organization to talk to each other no matter where they are around the country. This resource also allows people to pass documentation safely to each other in many forms in real-time. This source can be provided in both stationary and mobile formats.

There are many more technological resources readily available for entrepreneurs and business owners. Just about every need, demand or desire can be met in one way or another through various applications, software and hardware.

(9)   Work hard, but smart, persevere and remain flexible & adaptable

Every effort of an entrepreneur is normally defined by hard work, but working smart is the strategic method that all should adopt in their processes. In an entrepreneur's journey, you should make certain each step, each measure of movement is cautiously executed. Each entrepreneur will have their host of challenges, obstacles and roadblocks they will encounter at all levels and throughout their entire journey to success. Always be prepared that as you climb each level of success, there will be counter challenges. Always maintain a strong presence of determination and no matter what "bus hits you, runs over you", this is analogous to persevere and not to give up your dream, your quest for success. It may take more than you can possibly imagine to get through the bulk of your challenges, but know that the benefit of succeeding is much, much greater than any challenge can come your way.

Always remain consistent in your drive toward success, but streamline so that you can adjust to any situation fluidly. In the world of business, always remain flexible so that you can adjust to the rigid, traditional process of public sector business. When things shift from stress-free to maximum pressure, remain adaptable so that your adjustment to handle the situation transitions smoothly and with agility.

(10) **Work from a support structure of relevance to align your goals**

Most entrepreneurs, while creating their business plan, model, concepts, strategies, teams, staff, resources and other tasks don't normally think about their support structure. A support structure is like a building being designed, developed and built on a great piece of land that has been surveyed, prepared and excavated properly. When a General Contractor lays the foundation, they carefully design, research, calculate and ensure that the structure will within any environment, withstand load, weather, structure integrity and other technological events.

This is a similar approach that each entrepreneur should follow and incorporate into their structure plan. Most entrepreneurs are so focused on getting to the reward of business, making money and running fast to the prize of contract awards. They often don't realize that first, all entrepreneurs should spend time searching for structured platforms of organizational workshops, events and seminars that will produce a strong support structure for them.

Entrepreneurs should find a reliable support structure that provides the following:

- An organization that will continuously provide ongoing resources to help build their companies' certifications, policies, business platform, relationships and other resources.
- An organization that is continuously keeping up with technology and procedures.
- An organization to guide you to all of the basic knowledge you continuously need as day-to-day changes occur in your designated industry.
- A platform within an organization that has professionals that are advocating on your behalf.
- A group of professionals that are marketing on your behalf nationally so that you can utilize this platform as a base marker to illustrate your presence as a great foundation.
- An organization that supports small businesses, large businesses, government agencies, individuals, non-government agencies and that is designed to help you.
- A national organization if you are aiming for national business presence.

- An organization that you can determine that their top management has a similar focus that is aligned with your business goals.

Remember that as an entrepreneur, you should always connect with organizations, people and programs that always have your alignment of goals that you are pursuing in a similar format. In Government contracting, there are hundreds of organizations that provide many different resources to support your business. When choosing an organization, interview and research them to see if they meet and align with your goals of what you are trying to accomplish for your business.

(11) **Develop and associate yourself with a support network of individuals that will enhance your capabilities and abilities**

During your journey, make certain you develop a chain of supportive individuals that will support you in every area of your fierce entrepreneurial journey of business. Hopefully, prior to starting your business, you had already surrounded yourself with a group of individuals that you could count on during your business journey. Always measure every step of your entrepreneur/business process and have people around you that can bring added value to your arsenal of entrepreneurship.

Your Development:

Always ascertain, regardless of a person's achievements, that their values are equal to yours or perhaps greater. Regardless of how successful society has deemed a person to be, as you develop a friend or business associate, make certain that they align with your values both personally and professionally.

You should develop a set of guidelines that measure the attributes of the people you need to surround yourself around as it relates to your business. This means family members, friends, associates, mentors and advisors. The worst thing you can do is expose yourself to someone that is pushing for the opposite (failure) as it pertains to your journey.

Some related attributes should consist of the following as illustrated throughout this book for business, people, systems, etc.:

Balance of Life
Beliefs
Common Interest of Success
Faith
Level of Achievement
Loyalty
Trust
Values

You can and should test people around you to see what measures they bring to your journey. Some tests should involve things such as assessing their loyalty, sincerity and willingness to support you. See how they react when you expose them to unsuccessful events over time.

Your support network should be comprised of professional individuals of business of the highest integrity and family and friends that are comprised of the highest familial values that you can measure. You should attach to people that can bring added values to your business network. In your support network, you should include what I call the "Three Step System (TSS.)"

(1)   include people that will comprise the internal workings of your business,

(2)   include people that will enhance, structure and build your business from an external standpoint and

(3)   include people that will bring added value to you from an advisory standpoint, mentoring approach and "Business Building Model Concept (BBMC.)"

Always ensure that these professionals, whether business, family or friends, bring positive influence to your life, including your journey of entrepreneurship. If at any time you feel that a person is questionable to your cause of success, by my experience, take them out of your equation of success. Do not include a person in your entrepreneurial journey that illustrates a value towards failure of your targeted mission. Most of all, you should be flexible in taking people out of your journey if there's reason to believe they may cause havoc to your plan for success.

By my Faith in God, He provided me with my Entrepreneurship journey and when I stayed the course of His direction, I achieved great success and received great knowledge from my failures. You see, your support network should be a group of professionals of all types. These individuals should be an inner and outer layer of solutions for your success path and a solution for your failures to come. We all, whether we will admit it or not, receive failure in small and large ways I truly believe that your support network structure can either add to your success or failure . . . plan your network carefully.

(12) <u>**Gather all resources needed to accomplish what you set out to do**</u>

Most entrepreneurs get caught up in planning resources visually. I truly know that you should gather resources that seem transparent to us all. When gathering resources, include the visual items such as:

* Business Plan (Roadmap)
* Financial Plan
* Teaming Plan (normally the lack of for most businesses attributes to failure)
* Marketing Plan
* Business Development Plan
* Scope
* Concept Model
* Execution Model
* Political Model
* System Development Model
* Strategic Plan
* Tactical Plan
* Resource Plan

These are normally common, but 98% of businesses I have evaluated do not have the completeness of these plans and models. Even though some businesses are successful, they lack a great deal of these items which cause a great deal of unnecessary expenses that otherwise could be used in a more productive manner.

Now here is a list of non-transparent resources that add a tremendous amount of impact to your success as follows:

- TEAMING
- ADVISORY BOARD
- NATIONAL/INTERNATIONAL NETWORK
- LEGAL TEAM
- EXECUTIVE PROTECTION

Believe it or not, but as I dealt with thousands of businesses and their entrepreneurs from Fortune 100, 500 and small businesses, the ones that illustrated success for long-term results had all five items above and were connected with other teaming partners that had like resources.

Regardless how good we think we are in business, we can't do it alone, but we have to do it carefully and strategically with others in an "OBT Teaming" manner. "OBT Teaming" is very important and I will discuss it in more depth in latter chapters. As a matter of fact, "OBT Teaming" is so important to an entrepreneur's journey that one of my next set of books will be dedicated solely to "Teaming."

Discuss success/failure/distractions

Line of Success of Failure: Which Path will you take!

Don't follow these paths of Failure

"OBT STRATEGIC TEAMING"

Diagram 4-1

Earlier in Chapter 4, we discussed the "Measure of Success." Now I will discuss the "Illusions" and "Factors" of success. I will discuss the different "Phases of Success" that an Entrepreneur and Business Owner will face in their journey. Also, I will define "Failures" by direct obstacles or barriers relating to the art of "Distraction."

Illusions in the way of business success can cause an overwhelming failure for your business. It can cause you to go directly or indirectly off track and ultimately, to a road to disruption. Below you will see several definitions that I will use to explain how you need to overcome failure and distractions from false phases of success.

The different definitions of *"Illusion:"*

WEBSTER DICTIONARY:	
<ul><li>State or fact of being intellectually deceived or misled. MISAPPREHENSION: an instance of such deception.</li><li>Perception of something objectively existing in such a way as to cause misinterpretation of its actual nature. HALLUCINATION: a pattern capable of reversible perspective.</li></ul>	<ul><li>Misleading image presented to the vision. Something that deceives or misleads intellectually.</li><li>Conception or image created by the imagination and having no objective reality.</li><li>A false idea or belief.</li></ul>
There are many different definitions, but for the purpose pertaining to business situations, an entrepreneurial journey and overall business lifecycle I will only discuss related topics.	

There are many successful results that you will receive throughout your journey that you will be able to use to measure the levels of success you wish to reach. Be very thorough in your process, and create a system of fact finding to overcome the many illusions.

Here are several "illusions" to take into consideration along with "Factors" to counter: *(See Diagram 4-1)*

- **Illusion:** On many occasions wrong information is intentionally distributed between Entrepreneurs, Small Business Owners and others to divert their direction to success for their own gain.

- o **Factors:** Always check to ensure facts are true and valid. Never assume.
- **Illusion:** Frequently, Entrepreneurs and Small Business Owners will speak of having a particular Teaming Partner of substantial success or status which may be true. However, there may be some individuals who overstate their actual relationship with these partners. Ultimately, they want to get to that particular Entrepreneur or Small Business Owner's Teaming Partner, so they create a false sense of friendship to try to wrongfully penetrate their resources.
  - o **Factors:** Do not immediately accept friendships from strangers until they have earned the relationship of truly being a friend. (*See Chapter 9*)
- **Illusion:** Websites, fact sheets, brochures, pamphlets, presentations and a host of other marketing materials that look great, but really has no reality or substance to it.
  - o **Factors:** Validate all information that is verifiable.
- **Illusion:** An Entrepreneur or Small Business Owner that approaches others with the impression that they are ready to do business, have their entire business plan complete and that they are the sole decision-maker for their business when this is absolutely not true by way of them having business partners with equal decision rights in the business.
  - o **Factors:** There are many fact-checking processes to ensure that a business is ready to do business such as checking certifications. If possible, ask to see their business plan and check their business corporation entity status along with the authority of leadership and ownership.

- **Illusion:** When a company representative states that they represent the company with "fullness of authority," when in reality they have not even spoken with the true upper management for approval.
  - **Factors:** Always make certain you speak with all authority figures of a company for total buy-in on all decisions. Obtain a signed agreement in person if possible. If not, obtain signatures and recap with an electronic method (email) directly from that authority figure.
- **Illusion:** Through mentoring, a protégé is highly eager to be mentored to the point when they reach success level, then they immediately switch to another mentor to illustrate a total misrepresentation of integrity and loyalty.
  - **Factors:** Always get a pledge of commitment from everyone in writing. Even with the signed agreement, always place measures that will retain great value of resources so that if they break the integrity or loyalty. You do not lose all served and they do not totally gain everything by ending the commitment to earlier as agreed.

Your "Phases of Success (PHS)" should contain a clear vision, so you know you are climbing the vertical levels of success and not going backwards. The phases should be interlinked to make a complete series or process. This is important since you want to avoid every illusion, source of failure, barrier, obstacle and distraction.

Here are a few phases of success:

- Build your foundation to support your business structure. You can test the strength of knowledge of your foundation by comparison to other successful companies.
- Build your business structure with a strategic platform of interlinking information that will produce benefits without having to use monetary resources to accomplish the mission.
- Build and align your structure to provide a creative means of results. You can test this by sampling it into the market for awards of achievement.
- Put your strategies, methodologies and processes in place for your business. You can review others' success and mirror to your success.
- There are many other phases of success that you can use from the beginning of your business to the continuous building of your success and sustainment.

You will encounter many distractions that are normally temporary, but they can still cause adverse effects that can lead to failure. Distractions can appear in many forms, both directly and indirectly. One important way to overcome distractions is to take them head-on. Do not let them hang around unresolved because they will gradually turn into even bigger problems. Address them with full attention and do not take them for granted no matter how small or simple they may seem.

Here are a few distractions to watch out for:

- Non-executed documentation
- Unsupported documents that do not properly support a cause of a legal status
- Untrustworthy people
- Contracts that are out of reach based on your ability to support that contract. You waste time pursuing it only because you get attracted to the dollar amounts.
- Supported paperwork with deadlines that need your immediate attention, but you put it off which can slow or hinder your business process. Address all business deadlines accordingly.
- Make certain you get agreements, non-disclosures agreements (NDA), contracts, arrangements and other legal documents from licensed Attorneys and execute all said documents with signatures from all parties and have a witness to validate. (Notary or other witnesses of trust.)
- Be careful once the media or some other source catches wind of your success. This will place you in the public, so do not get caught up in the fame; just stay grounded. Also, always check the motive of that particular media outlet or organization's intentions to make certain your interests are protected.

Discuss strategies, methodologies, processes and procedures to forward your concept into reality.

In order for your company to be successful, you will need strategies, methodologies, processes and procedures to accomplish your business mission. You hear in the marketplace about so many business failures, closures and legal matters that occur. This happens because of the non-existence or lack of strategies, methodologies, processes and procedures. The businesses that succeed have a blend of all.

Here are the definitions of Methodology, Procedure, Process and Strategy to give you a better understanding of the importance of reasoning to forward your concept into reality:

- Methodology—a body of methods and rules followed in a discipline.
- Procedure—a particular way of doing something. A series of steps followed in a particular order.
- Process—a series of actions or operations directed toward a particular result. Progress or Advancement.
- Strategy—a careful plan or method for achieving an end.

Remember to do your due diligence when constructing your system of operational structure.

Here are a few helpful tips that should tremendously help you in your business flow and impact your business success:

First—Always generate your methodologies to create your rules of engagement. You have to create an ordered type of business.

Second—Always create your procedures to develop the ordered rules designed for your business scope within multi-layers of business flow structure.

Third—In your planning, you have to develop a well-organized and defined series of techniques in a strategic and tactical manner to be highly prepared to achieve your end results.

Fourth—The three mentioned steps are not complete until you have actions behind it. You have to implement the process which is the driving machine of action and execution.

Here is a formula to remember:

(Methodology + Procedure) + Strategy + Process = SOOS (Strategic Order of Success™)

There are many ways of accomplishing a Strategic Order of Success™, from personal experience I will provide you with a few successful examples that we have used and created that will help you in your entrepreneurial journey. These are proven by success, not theory.

- OBT Competitive Business Intelligence (OBTCBI™ or CBI™): Our process is well proven in the marketplace. Our developmental design is based on many parts that form a complete, strategic situation to engage in the process of gaining information to outdo our competitors.
- 3 Point Check System (OBT3PCS or 3PCS): As stated, most businesses only check once after completion of some type of process. Some check twice, but the ultimate goal of success is the third system check. This can be related to a Human Resources Interviewing Process, Proposal Submittal, Hiring Process, Relationship Building and any other check and balance as needed.

* Strategic Advisory Board (OBTSAB or SAB): This board can serve many purposes that provide unlimited resources. You should take time to create a strong board of experienced members that will add the greatest value to your business. Absolutely make certain that all alignments are connected through your business, associated Teaming Partners, Systems & Processes and all aspects of your business.

* **OBT Strategic Teaming™ (OBT Teaming™ or OBTS Teaming™):** While all of the processes of the Strategic Order of Success™ (SOOS) are extremely important, "OBT Strategic Teaming" is the most important. We have another name for this which is called "Credibility by Teaming™" or "Credibility by OBT Teaming™." There are so many advances built into this process that I have another book being published soon called **"OPERATION BREAKTHROUGH: Credibility by Teaming™."**

Here are a few unlimited resources:

  o Multi-Functional Team (OBTMFT or MFT)
  o Multi-Functional Process (OBTMFP or MFP)
  o Multi-Functional Strategy (OBTMFS or MFS)
  o Multi-Level Business Development (OBTMLBD or MLBD)
  o Multi-Level Marketing (OBTMLM or MLM)
  o Multi-Level Structure Building (OBTMLSB or MLSB)
  o Multi-Level Competitive Advancement (OBTMLCA or MLCA)

- ○ Multi-Level Competitive Intelligence (OBTMLCI or MLCI)
- ○ Multi-Level Opportunity Building (OBTMLOB or MLOB)
- ○ Much more

You should always develop your plan of action to face the realities of your business goals. Always stay ahead of the changing times of technology, economic landscape, politics and industry contracts by embedding cutting edge tools into your array of strategies. A means of expanding your strategic teaming is a means to broadening your ability to be successfully diversified. Remember, building a business is like building a house. You do not construct a house without first laying a foundation that consists of piers, reinforcement bars and various other materials or the house will not be balanced, structured properly and gradually, it will fall. You do not construct the structure (framing, flooring, walls, ceilings, electrical, plumbing, etc.) without the foundation. You do not construct the roof on a structure until it is strongly and properly sound. You then add the shingles, roof ventilator and other materials to keep the weather from destroying the structure and the contents within the house. There is a series of inspections that must be accomplished at every step to ensure quality and functionality meets the satisfaction of codes and regulations. If this does not happen, then it will not pass inspection. To build a home correctly logistically, you have to put together a team of professionals that are skilled, certified, experienced and knowledgeable in their trade or profession. Would you build your home without the proper resources? If you wouldn't, why build your business without the proper resources? This is why most businesses fail. They try to take the shortcut either with their resources or they just do not understand the logistical process of building. Do you know what it takes to build a business? Which path of building will you take for your business?

Determine your cost effectiveness, necessary expenses and time expectations for success.

COST EFFECTIVENESS

This is an extremely important set of processes that determine the growth, spending and outcome of your business. Determining the cost value of your services or products can be one of the most challenging events that will take place during your business process. You have to research extensively in order to understand your cost positioning in your perspective marketplace.

There are many different sourcing methods to accomplish your proper cost breakdowns to make certain you correctly cost out your services, products and means for doing business as follows:

- Review historical and current cost factoring data charts that you can access free through USASpending.gov.
- Check and compare competitor pricing.
- Check trend pricing from related contracts based on your services and products.
- Extremely understand your industry (internal and external) and its surroundings.
- Review market demand for 10 years prior and projected pricing for your product and services.

What is Cost Effectiveness in Business? The ability to reach your level of success by means of making certain that a business makes more money than it spends. This can be accomplished by maximizing income and by minimizing output. Methods of cost effectiveness help business owners to meet the needs of their businesses at the lowest possible cost. The challenge is to acquire superior resources, staff and facilities without spending so much that profit margins are affected. Be very strategic in your quest to maximize cost effectiveness by implementing the following:

- Always validate the best price for everything at the highest quality.
- Always strive for cost savings.
- Generate relationships that have resource advantages.
- Generate innovative techniques for cost containment.
- Buy a large volume of various business items to achieve cost savings.
- Teaming can be an unlimited resource for maximum cost savings.

NECESSARY EXPENSES

Another important way to maximize cost effectiveness is to smartly deal with your necessary expenses. Expenses can be challenging on any business type. It is very difficult to limit expenses, but the key is to define the necessary expenses. What are the necessary expenses related to your business? There are many different types of expenses that you will encounter for your business, so it is important to differentiate from unnecessary expenses. Listed below are necessary and unnecessary expenses, but each business will differ in its business needs and wants:

Necessary Expenses:

- Branding
- Business Certifications
- Business Development
- Business Licenses
- Business Planning
- Competitive Intelligence
- Computers/Laptops
- Database(s)
- Employee Benefits
- Marketing
- Office
- Office Equipment
- Payroll
- Relationship Building
- Research
- Software/Hardware
- Travel

Unnecessary Expenses:

- Excessive office space
- Traditional office space
- Traditional phone system
- Unnecessary business equipment
- Unnecessary Certifications

- Unnecessary Licenses
- Unnecessary Travel

TIME EXPECTATIONS

Another important limitation that can impact your ability to achieve success is "Time Expectation." You have to be very precise in your movement of business development and transitioning towards your path to success. Make certain you prepare your entire business timeline to meet the milestones of your business based on certain scenarios as such:

- Economic situations that may impact your business directly or indirectly.
- Political issues that can be of value or hindrance to your business.
- Industry changes and trends that may affect your business.
- Market segmentation

In determining your time expectations for success, you want to make sure you observe and strategically protect yourself from various degrees of obstruction. Technically, you have to prepare your arsenal of business tools, processes and methodologies to support many different scenarios of obstruction as follows:

- When speaking to others always, engage your conversations to measure the proper time release of selective information for various reasons:
  - From experience, you can release business information to people that may support your efforts that can forward it to the market for greater impact to success.

- o On the other hand, you can release certain disjointed business information to people with the unforeseen bad intentions to eliminate your path to success. It is very timely to implement this action.
- A Business Partner that has the same initial, strategic ambitions, but is not willing to actually take the total challenge because of a lack of sweat equity or commitment vested into the business.

Obstruction can come in many forms:

- Advisory Board Members
- Board of Directors/Members
- Business Partners
- Investors
- Leeches (We all know these types—people who only want your success and do not have intentions of creating their own.)
- Some people are short-fused for success and if they have money tied into the business, they can become extremely impatient about the proper timing of success.
- Timing for business transformation

Remember to determine your necessary expenses immediately so that you can create cost effectiveness in a timely manner. This is very important to get to your journey of success.

Entrepreneurs and Small Business Owners have to decide at the beginning of their business process to be extremely patient and always take in consideration time measurements to success.

Analyze and access businesses that have succeeded and ones that have failed.

How do you avoid going out of business? Prior to even beginning your business, always research businesses that have reached success and adopt their innovative methodologies and processes. Find out how they overcame obstacles and challenges. Determine their time span to success and most importantly, try to find out their downfalls along the way. Define the details of the working models they used to accomplish success.

It is extremely important to strategically gather as much data as possible on all the businesses that have failed, but most importantly, how they failed. You want to create what we call a "Data Failure Chart (DFC.)" This chart will provide you with many different levels and types of failed business processes and methodologies. You want to create this because it will eliminate your chances of failure. The more that's known about prior failures, the more you will add value to creating a successful logic. This may be time consuming, but look at the overall value this will bring to your business development. Don't take a shortcut to success.

Determine your space in the market sector for growth and sustainability.

Build your business with "Economic Strategies or OBT Economic Strategies™" that will allow you to become knowledgeable about your business positioning in the market. You should determine a continuous, competitive advantage point of your business in the marketplace by analyzing your market segment both today and in the future. In the world of business, changes occur daily so you have stay current to make certain your business makes the necessary changes to move you in the direction of success. Always make certain you understand the politics that surround your business developmental process today and tomorrow. In your planning, always construct your structure and business system for economic issues or policies to make sure you are aligned for success.

Review industry data that relates to your business to adjust to the advantages of building growth. Gather information continuously on innovative tools to advance growth and generate a strategic business model that allow you to achieve continuous business strength especially that targets your market position.

The "Art of OBT Teaming™" will allow you many innovative ways to create strategic means to accomplish your growth and sustainability. Within your teaming model, always build an "Advisory Board" to help achieve your growth, market segment and business position in the market.

Develop the pre-strategic small business solution by OBTS methodology.

Our Pre-Strategic Small Business Solution is developed through our unique methodology known as "Strategic Teaming to Tactical Success (STTS)" or "OBTS Teaming". Our proven innovative, multiple series of methodologies provide multi-layers of interlinking processes that extend throughout your entire business journey. It is composed of a proven structure of success and rooted in a solid foundation, strategic support structure, alignment of unlimited strategic collaborators, adapted to changes of the industry and flexible enough to adjust to success driven by business changes.

We have helped many small, medium and large sized businesses with building a successful business model.

Our methodology provides a host of unlimited resources that provide pre-strategic processes such as:

- Business Position Building
- Generational Growth
- Horizontal & Vertical Support
- Innovative Resources
- Interlinking Reinforcement
- Market Segmentation Solutions
- Strategic Foundation
- Tactical Business Resolutions
- Tactical Market Techniques
- Technical Teaming Partners
- And much more

Make certain that you adopt or create some type of pre-strategic small business solution to avoid the downfalls of business. Don't rely on guessing your way through the business maze because ultimately, you will find yourself at the end of your business journey prior to accomplishing any success. This normally results in failure with a great financial loss. Don't repeat the cycle of disappointment.

Chapter 5

The Root and Building of the OBTS Structure!

Determine principles (business & character) and the culture (business & character) of your structure.

Your business structure can't be complete without the infrastructure of principles and the culture of the business. Let's discuss the infrastructure of principles relating to your business structure. Your principles should contain the three (3) T's (Think, Technical and Tactical—**TTT**) which capture the elements of business. These elements should provide the rules or code of conduct that solely define business and leadership character of your structure. You should make certain to incorporate the **TTT** element levels of your business. Whatever you do, please commit 100% to building your structure and your entrepreneurial business journey will be that much smoother. Below are the principles of business and character needed for your structure while implementing **TTT** as follows:

- The <u>Principles</u> of your business structure should be well-designed, determined and developed to achieve maximum intellectual strength.
  - o THINK: <u>The business principles</u> should be defined thoroughly with a vast amount of analytical rationale. Each element should be interlinked with collaborated infrastructure. <u>The character principles</u> of your business structure should contain uniformity and diversity of leadership. It should be composed of the highest caliber of business reputation and built-in **"Credibility by Teaming™."**
  - o TECHNICAL: <u>The business principles</u> should be designed with innovative logic that define the strategic support to the structure. It should be connected to the foundation of your business as well as the pathways to your business success to the top. <u>The character principles</u> of your business structure should contain loyalty, integrity and trust at every aspect of infrastructure of professionals.
  - o TACTICAL: <u>The business principles</u> should be designed with connecting segments of strategies interlinked with protective measures embedded in your structure. <u>The character principles</u> of your business structure should contain overlapping trust mechanisms of aligned specialty professionals that have total common interest of success by way of collaboration. Again, we call this **"Credibility by Teaming™."**

There has to be another very important part of the structure that works simultaneously with the business principles and that is the Culture of the business. Without this important segment, you will have an unsupported structure. Below are the principles of business and character needed for your structure using the **TTT** as follows:

- The <u>Culture</u> of your business structure should be designed per the culture of your leadership. It should be built with the highest standards of trust, loyalty, diverse traits, flexibility, adaptation and certitude.
  - THINK: <u>The culture principles</u> of business and leadership character should be diversely designed with the highest standards of indistinguishable, personal, positive traits within the leaders of the business structure.
  - TECHNICAL: <u>The culture principles</u> of business and character structure should be designed with "check & balance" systems to maintain the highest integrity.
  - TACTICAL: <u>The culture principles</u> of business and character should be defined by the total business cycle with all professionals involved of equal integrity.

Fully commit to your business structure and adhere to all aspects of the highest standards of professionalism. Do not compromise in any areas of your business structure or it will crack rapidly because of business obstacles.

Determine the below & above foundation of your business (Inverted Upside Triangle Effect™ or IUTE™) with anchors.

Before exploring and conquering your business success, you will want to first create a strong foundation to support your business. Your foundation should contain at a minimum the following:

Below Foundation:

- Extensive amount of business industry research
- Extensive due diligence of your business position in the marketplace
- Gathering of collaborated teaming partners with the same ambitions, but most importantly, common characteristics of professionalism
- Common interest of goal settings
- Common interest of determination

Above Foundation:

- Determination of trusted professionals prior to commencing business
- Gathering or development of innovative methodologies and processes
- Business Model for forecasting an ideal, reachable position in the market
- Refinement and decisive teaming partner collaboration
- Generational growth alignment based on collective agreements

Most Entrepreneurs and Small Business Owners operate their businesses with the illusion, yes, illusion that they are climbing a ladder of success on a sloped triangle to this great apex to the top. Don't get caught up like the many failed businesses that chased the top of success by cutthroat actions, wrongful intentions to others and lack of knowledge of the business. When this occurs, a habit of leeching occurs. Leeching is when one or more businesses attach to others to gain their processes of success only to gain for themselves. Stay away from these kind of entrepreneurs or small business owners.

The most successful move to success is to create an "Inverted Upside Down Triangle™" and follow all the procedures associated. This is the most effective way of business success. Why do most businesses disregard this method?

There are many reasons listed below:

- Can't see the vision
- Do not want to accomplish the intense and lengthy homework.
- Do not want to share the wealth.
- Do not want to take on the due diligence.
- Lack of discipline
- Lack of knowledge

Remember no business can accomplish success alone. From Fortune 100, 500 to 1000 businesses, you can research and find that the majority of these businesses never accomplished success by themselves. A Question to all Entrepreneurs and Small Business Owners: What makes you think you can accomplish success on your own?

An **"Inverted Upside Down Triangle™"** is positioned so that when you reach success, you would have gotten there with many other partners. This form of methodology can provide many great resources such as:

- Ability to reduce spending
- Credibility to contracts
- Credibility to the Industry
- Reduction of problems
- Increased number of Teaming Partners with integrity
- Resource gain without cost
- Many more

Anchors, as we call them, are an interlinking line of businesses that support themselves in a reciprocating manner from the entire business cycle, from the foundation to the top of the success ladder.

Formula for Success

Great Foundation + Great Structure + Vast Amount of Resources + Numerous Amount of Strategic Teaming Partners = **FORMULA FOR SUCCESS (FFS)**

Build your business structure to withstand all types of adversities (obstacles, barriers, struggles, etc.) and your levels of success will physically arrive by the vision of your entrepreneurial dreams.

Determine your alignment by Structure, by Mentors (unofficial first, then official if possible), by Teaming, by Partners and by Business Opportunities.

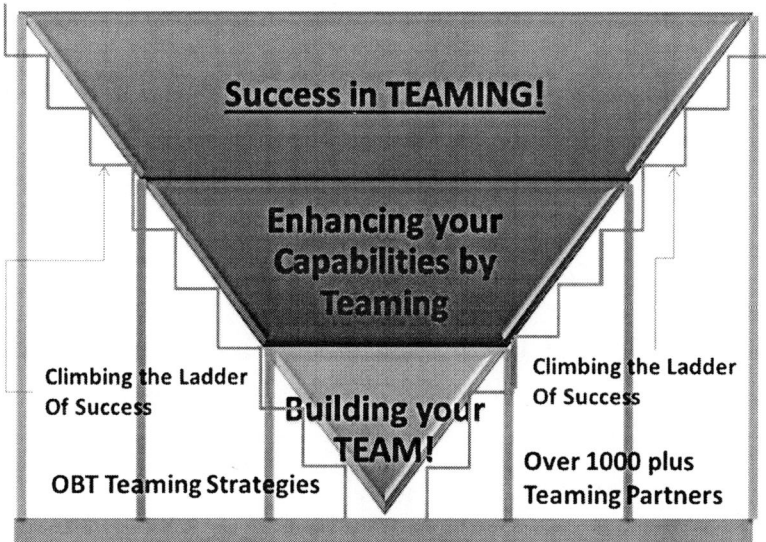

Success in TEAMING!

Enhancing your Capabilities by Teaming

Climbing the Ladder Of Success

Building your TEAM!

OBT Teaming Strategies

Climbing the Ladder Of Success

Over 1000 plus Teaming Partners

Teaming Partners from the Bottom to Success!

"Strenthening as you Climb the Ladder of Success"

ALIGNMENT BY STRUCTURE

Every aspect of your business should have connecting paths of alignment. It has to start from the foundation of the structure continuing through the entire business system. Whether you decide not to or merely do not have an understanding to add alignment to your overall business, either way you will set yourself up for failure. Don't take a shortcut thinking that you can save time because ultimately, you would have paid a tremendous cost in restructuring to get alignment. Most Entrepreneurs & Small Business Owners think that structure is just merely your particular business in general. Your structure is defined by many sub-structures. There are too many to cover in this one book, but I will highlight the most important ones for your structure alignment.

Here is a list of some structures sub-structures of alignment:

- The building block of your business is the foundation. You have to build this platform to withstand the core and structure of your business. This is the core nucleus of your inner team (business plan, staff, standards, guidelines, models, etc.)
- Your structure is anchored in the foundation by the pillars, beams, reinforcement, piers, etc. which represent your methodologies, processes and Teaming Partners and built to withstand the verticals of your business.
- The verticals of your business should be totally aligned to the marketplace you are targeting for business.
- You should gain as many business certifications as possible that relates to your core business services or products.

Your structure should be designed like our inverted triangle of business above. Your alignment by structure should interlink with your alignment by mentors. This is very tricky because many times, you will not have an official mentor, so you find unofficial ones to complete your alignment by mentors.

ALIGNMENT BY MENTORS

You should be very critical in this process of your business. You can't assume because someone is successful in either your related or non-related business industry that they should be your mentor. Mentors are sometimes hard to find because the mentor's character should be similar to your own character. It is sometimes difficult to measure the character of the person you want to pursue because the success of that individual is normally overpowering the character attributes by that person's appearance. This is why you have to try to get to know these individuals in a more personal rather than professional way. It is probably a better situation to create an unofficial mentorship first, so that you can make certain that the total character of the mentor surfaces before a formal commitment of an official mentorship is locked in. Keep in mind that you can just go and get the commitment of the person you want to be mentored by. The potential mentor may not want to take part in a mentorship or maybe they may not want to mentor you. Whatever the case maybe, once they are approached by you for mentorship, they will conduct an extensive checklist to be met by their requirements. Mentorship is a huge responsibility and commitment. It can cost a lot of money and time depending on location, type of commitment and time expectations. You have to have extensive reasons as to why you want to be mentored and what will it benefit both in the short and long term of your personal and business journey of business. Mentorships should be sought out for professional, spiritual and the character building aspects of your entrepreneurial journey. You have to open your mind and be able to take advice which may come in the form of "criticism."

Through my experience of pursuing mentors, I can tell you that it can be accomplished in many ways. Remember that you can achieve the same results in an official or non-official method. When you are determining your mentorship, it is not actually necessary for them to have a business background the exact same as yours. You should seek mentorships in other areas of business (internal and external) and to strengthen your character, management, leadership, creative and innovative thinking.

Here are a few ways to determine your mentorship alignment:

- Make certain your mentor has the experience and knowledge of your business industry.
- Make absolute sure that their personality matches with yours.
- Make certain that the mentorship will add value to your business.

Remember the objectives for mentorship is to:

- further educate yourself,
- advance your all-around knowledge of business,
- advance your personal character traits,
- provide business advice,
- place people around that can bring added value and resources and

- most importantly, to think long-term, you should desire the source of "Credibility."

This brings me to the next subject matter and a very important part of determination of alignment which is "Teaming" or "Alignment by Teaming."

ALIGNMENT BY TEAMING

"Teaming" or **"OBT Teaming™"** is the entire inner and outer workings of our business model which demands a great deal of alignment. But if you spend the time and effort to develop the alignment correctly and strategically, you will create unlimited resources, solutions, business processes and a thorough business modeling set of concepts.

Here are a few of many ways to determine your teaming alignment:

- Make certain you get teaming partners that add value to your business, but who can build mutual trust at every aspect of your business.
- Make certain that any teaming partner you form a relationship with is aligned with your business goals.
- Make certain that you add value to your teaming partners' business model and possess common interest of mutual business success.
- Example: When forming your teaming alignment with a large company, don't go to them unprepared. Make certain you understand the common benefit of the mutual teaming alignment and understand their business interests.
- Understand the economic limitations of the alignment.

ALIGNMENT BY PARTNERS

- Fully know your potential partner's ambition—goals of ownership—"Level of Success" and "Expectations." False or incorrect knowledge can carry you completely away from your success track.
- Make certain legal documents are executed for agreements, non-disclosure agreements (NDAs) and other documents needed to conduct business.
- Build a long-term relationship. Stay away from the short-term relationships.
- Stay aware of people wanting to immediately team with you when they don't know you.
- Never place yourself into a teaming situation that is not properly vetted. For example, never place yourself into a database of teaming prospects to just merely gain opportunities together. Get to know them personally prior to doing business together.
- Never think that teaming is just merely two companies working together without a relationship. This will cause lots of problems in the short-term.
- Prior to doing business, meet with your potential teaming partners at non-business related events to see how they react. Example: In a restaurant, when ordering lunch or dinner together, without your teaming partner's knowledge, have the waitress or waiter slightly change their order on purpose to see how they react. If they are polite, then they probably are of good character. If they react in anger, this will illustrate a huge lack of customer service skills. You may want to stay away from these types of individuals.

ALIGNMENT BY BUSINESS OPPORTUNITIES

If you have completely developed your alignment of structure, mentors, teaming and partners, then your pursuit of alignment for opportunities will be less complex. The process of credibility extends deeply in the achievement of opportunities. If you have your business alignment processes out of sync or it merely doesn't exist, then you will not be in the correct position to pursue your business opportunities. Your ability of receiving business opportunities will null or void.

Imagine an airplane taking off the runway or landing and you are the pilot. Every step in your process is critical in your order of take-off or landing to be successful.

Imagine constructing a building. You would start from the footing, foundation to structure, interior and exterior. But the completion would extend far beyond the walls of the interior and everything inside.

Imagine going into battle, you would never go into battle without the proper equipment and a well though-out action plan or battle plan.

The question to all! In business like the examples mentioned above. Why do most entrepreneurs or small business owners think that in order to gain business opportunities they just have to see their product or service and the potential clients just need to buy them? Well, think again, because you have to define every intricate step in your process of pursuing business opportunities.

You have to make sure that you position your business relationships to a level of credibility, build the proper type relationships and always cultivate them periodically. Most importantly, make certain your business service offerings or products provide a great benefit to your potential or targeted clients' organization. If you strategically provide every step of the way factual supporting information to justify your service offerings or products in their organization to produce a "cost savings" or "profit" solution then you will succeed in your sell of your service offerings or products.

If you prove that the capability of your service offerings, products or solutions is more than adequate of the average services that may have obtained in the past, then you have just provided a great external alignment for business opportunities. If your potential clients fully understand your service offerings, products or solutions engaged in their organization as a great benefit and they clearly see the transition as a smooth operational cost saving method, then you have just created a great internal source of business alignment. When this occurs, effectively you have accomplished your internal and external measures to capture your targeted business opportunities. This is what the alignment is all about. What measures will you take in your pursuit of business alignment?

As you define your alignment for your business opportunities you will notice that your success or failure to create the proper alignment will be driven by the strength and design of your teaming model. Logically you should define your layers of structure to interlink and have a proven method of success that provides a source of future business advancements.

Strategically, every mentor you have should possess a process of added value towards your alignment for business opportunities.

This will provide you with forward intelligence for your alignment to produce advance internal resources for your strategy of pursuit of business opportunities.

Strategically, your teaming partners should play a vital alignment indirectly or directly with your potential clients. Their source of great business relationships with your potential clients will provide a streamline source of credibility that you can't place a valuable on towards success.

Build with strategic global awareness even if not global. ECONOMY: (Think big with small details in mind and your outcome will always be the above-targeted goals.)

Small Business Owners have to be very creative and innovative in the changing economic times of today, tomorrow and further in the future. As an Entrepreneur and Small Business Owner, you must always build your business with the mindset of thinking strategically about global awareness even if not in the pursuit of global business. You have to think big with small, innovative details in mind. You may have heard the expression, "if you are jumping upward, aim for the sky;" well, it's the same with business. You are aiming for a certain level of success, so aim much higher than your set goals.

You have to keep abreast of the changing situations that may impact the economy globally as related to your industry directly. You should maintain knowledgeable of other industries that may impact your business in either a direct or indirect way.

Whether in business, working in Corporate America or globally, you must remain politically correct at all times, but you still have to speak your mind. Do it strategically to get your point across.

Build your OBTS Structure with strategic design extension with both lateral support and upward support.

We know from a structural design of our business model, we have experienced a great deal of success at every milestone of our business. We have received awards and recognitions prior to even winning any contracts. We attracted other business types (WOSB, VOSB, HUB ZONE, SDVOSB, MOSB, 8A, etc. and small, medium and large businesses) for support because we had validated success in the marketplace. By the time we reached a substantial level of contract winnings as Prime Contractor and subcontract winnings from our Teaming Partners, we had proven that our methodology was driven to be of great success in any industry, product or service offerings. Once we had achieved a Teaming Partnership/Teaming Alliance commitment with every business regardless of size, we knew that our approach was unique, innovative and most of all "successful." The biggest reason for the great success of our methodology was building our structure of business by "Credibility by Teaming" from total alignment to overall strategic design of "Extension Lateral Support (ELS)" and "Upward Strategic Support (USS.)"

The Extension Lateral Support by our standards, OBT Standards, is the foundation to the structure, structure to internal and external staff and the internal and external staff to the building processes interlinked to the Teaming Partners to achieve a total cycle of business collaboration for overall support.

The Upward Strategic Support by our OBT Standards is the "cross members" to "vertical members" of business building blocks to form steps of success by climbing in collaboration with the alignment of business partnering. When working towards the climb to success in our methodology, you gain support in every aspect of your business journey. You are never alone in your climb to success. When you fall short of your mark, there is a lateral and upward support chain. Now, will you still have the mindset to do business on your own or will you adopt the OBT Strategic Teaming™ method?

Use your Internal and External Intelligence now for marketing, branding, business development, contracting, quality acceptance of your methodology-process-approach and structuring your business. Don't cut corners. Take the full journey to success.

PART V

STRATEGIC BREAKTHROUGH!

PENETRATION / FORWARD INTELLIGENCE!

Chapter 6

The Preparation, Alignment, Approach before launch!

Positioning before Pursuit

Always build from the ground upward and outward with your business and ensure that every segment of your business is connected and interlinked as stated in the previous chapters. After you have completed your total overall business model composed of your methodologies and processes, you should be ready for pursuit. I would say no, you are not ready at the moment.

Your positioning will be achieved when you have passed the testing of attraction of other businesses trying to duplicate your processes and once you have directly received the results of successful testing in the marketplace. We knew we were ready for the "Positioning" phase when we have accomplished all of our milestones of development and received invitations to be a "success story" for other organizations through the following:

- When we were placed in National to Global Contractor Business Guides for millions of other Entrepreneurs and

Small Business Owners to model and implement our **"OBT Strategic Teaming™"** methodology and processes.

- When we get one of the largest Financial Firms and the largest Government Contractors in the United States and the World to model our ideas, concepts and acknowledge our methodology as a proven successful resource for all businesses to model.
- When business entities and organizations of all sizes tried to steal or duplicate our idea or when many businesses offered us ownership of their businesses to merely have us connected to their businesses to obtain our reputation for credibility.
- When we, as a small business, attracted large Government and Private Sector Contractors to model and implement some of our processes.
- When an entity of the Department of Defense identified our methodology as a Business Model to implement and execute.
- When we captured unique "Teaming Partners" as "Subcontractors" such as the largest and most successful Fortune 100 and 500 large businesses of our Nation.

This is when you are ready since you have passed the test for positioning, so now the "Pursuit" phase should be ready for takeoff. What level of positioning have you built for your business and has it been tested?

Your ability to strategically commence the "Pursuit" of your business campaign should be approved by you. You should have tested, obtained direct or indirect approval by other business entities or organizations and adopted a full process of business flow to measure your aligned success. Here are the factors to check to ensure you have implemented in your business cycle model accordingly:

* Preparation
* Due Diligence
* Persistence for Business Alignment
* Positioning
* Full Processes and Methodologies

Now you have credibility in the marketplace to receive a favorable perception to achieve progress. This constitutes **"OBT Perception to Progress™—OBT PTP or PTP"** in our model. You are now ready for your next steps in your pursuit of business.

Interlinking Strategic Initial Success through Alignment

Don't get caught up in the perspective of things, but make certain that when you are ready to appear in the marketplace that your perspective of business is the best or at least one of the best in the industry. If you incorporated all the mentioned alignments stated in Chapter 5 and throughout the book, then your perspective reflects the readiness for business. When you achieve total alignment for all of your methodologies and processes, then you are ready to proceed to the business marketplace for branding and the first phase of business development.

Leap of Faith

Before stepping out into the industry, make certain you are ready in all areas of your business process. Don't get caught up in the false illusion of business. Don't start your business by selling your soul, meaning selling too much of your business to investors.

The Art of Distraction is known in the business industry, but not really understood. There are so many small businesses who believe that they are ready soon as they have a name for their business to launch out into the marketplace. They do not understand the importance of business structure, foundation, infrastructure, plan/roadmap and especially teaming. What happens is they just jump out into the challenging business marketplace and fail. What comes next is business closure before they even figured out what they needed to do to conduct business. The reason is that the industry is too complex and complicated. It is partially true that the industry is complex and complicated, but you can navigate through all of the distractions by developing your strategic leap of faith by understanding your footing in the marketplace. Will you take the leap of faith prepared or unprepared?

Keep your faith at high levels and don't let anyone deter you from your direction.

Entrepreneurship can be extremely fun, but can lend itself to a tremendous amount of stress, frustration, adversity, obstacles and disappointments. It is important that you keep your faith deeply rooted. You have to rely on a great deal of inner strength and motivation to drive through continuous struggles that come in your path of success. You have to be able to have thick skin, meaning you have to be able to take criticism and filter a lot of non-productive information from others that try to derail you from your success journey.

Whatever you do while being challenged by many different people, don't get taken out of your alignment by the comments that you hear directly or indirectly. Keep in mind that the majority of people will not understand your direction of where, what, why and how you need to target your business. Remember, your roadmap (business plan) is your plan of definitive direction. Unless others have your motivated, driven route, they will be confused about your business. They will still try to provide you with direction and if you take it, you will proceed in the wrong direction. I am not speaking of people such as your advisors or supporters that add great influence to your business, but I am speaking of people that want to lead you to where they think you should go which is most likely the wrong direction.

Remember, your roadmap will lead you to where you need to go to achieve your business success. A lot of people, including other entrepreneurs, like to provide information as to how entrepreneurs and small business owners should direct their business to succeed. Sometimes this can be good, but a lot of times this can create a disaster for your business. If you create your business structure from the beginning with the proper building blocks and guidelines, then you will be able to filter the right information to add to your roadmap. Research and do your homework to make certain you have factual information. Validate all information and filter positive files of storage for immediate or future use or file it in the "fault" storage so that you do not make that mistake of retaining false information.

I want to provide you with a few "points of interest" to beware of when people are eager to provide you with misguided information:

- Point of Interest 1: When people provide you with information, ask them if they have validated the information and if they can provide you with the point of reference.
- Point of Interest 2: Check, validate and approve all information.
- Point of Interest 3: Only allow reliable resources of information through people you deem credible.
- Point of Interest 4: Don't get caught up in a dead-end communication time zone. Don't continue to keep wasting time with people that provide you with non-relevant information.

Chapter 7

The Strategic Conference Performance

Planning for Preparation

While developing your entire planning process, detail-by-detail to attend various conferences, symposiums, procurement and other related business or networking events, always construct a plan of action to benefit your business and time constraints. If there is no benefit for your attendance to the event, then do not waste your time and money. If there is no absolute impact to success in a direct or indirect manner, then re-consider another event of greater value to add to your business. You may need to attend at another time when it will have a more meaningful impact on your business.

In preparing, consider the following benefits for your business attendance:

- Make certain that there is an organization, agency or business that you need to speak with at the event. But make certain you pre-arrange conversation with that entity prior to going so that the impact of your meeting time has great value.

- Schedule meetings with a decision-maker or someone that can benefit from your pursuit through their entity for procurement considerations.
- Conference Associated and Cost (CAC) versus Knowledge Business Advancement™ (KBA)
- Your core business alignment
- Advancement for your business
- Initial Pre-Networking or pre-planned networking arrangements
- Branding and Marketing
- Pre-Business Development
- Testing the marketplace with your products and/or services

Keep in mind that if you do not plan prior to going to a conference, then you will most likely achieve bad results. You may have great conversations, receive lots of great information and even get motivated, but after you get back from the conference, you will see the effects of non-productive results.

Planning your conference session attendance is essential. Think about how many sessions you will attend and how you will capture the information presented by the speakers. Will you take electronic notes on your device such as on an iPad, laptop, recorder or manually on paper? Will you take photos or video if you are able to do so? Do you know where or if you can get a copy of the speakers' presentations? Check to see if there is a speaker video capture so you can review later and share with your team.

Important things to do before and at a Conference:

- Read up on all materials about the conference, how it is structured, what breakout sessions are provided, and other related activities (breakfast, lunch, dinner, galas, and other events) that may occur at the conference.

* Show up prepared so that you maximize the true value from the conference.
* Listen up at the conference to the speakers, the audience, the flow of information, importance of the conference and the after action report of the conference.
* Follow up (most critical) after the conference. Discuss the outcome of the conference and if it was a great success for you. Identify other related conferences so that you can attend them.

Always come up with a process system that will bring added value to your business while attending a conference or related event.

* Think (Logic of Thought): Create an overall planning process to capture the innovative ideas to maximize the benefits of the conference.
* Technical (Strategic Informational Method (SIM)): Create a list of strategies to manage and direct your way through the conference to capture the optimal information available.
* Tactical ("Operation Breakthrough" or "Operational Structure Penetration" (OSP)): Create a series of procedures to use in dealing with the audience, conference exhibitors, speakers and procurement representatives.

Preparation for Purpose

There are innovative ways to optimize the business value of attending conferences. One way is defined by increasing your network's growth. In order for your business to be successful and to achieve credibility, you have to grow your network. There is no shortcut or substitution for developing a quality network; it takes quite a bit of time to grow a personal and professional network. Physically attending conferences and online networking events are essential for productive networking that can result in a variety of valuable outcomes including, but not limited to:

- Collecting competitive intelligence
- Consultant sourcing
- Marketplace awareness
- Marketplace innovation
- Prospecting for new clients
- Recruiting and Staffing
- Strategic Alignment & Growth
- Teaming Partner sourcing

When you attend conferences and events, set your goals for the type of contacts you want to make that relates to your industry. Build a list of people you want to meet if they're particularly important to your goals, but prior to going to the conference, attempt to send an initial email or place a phone call. Initiate new connections for your business alignment with qualified prospects of interest, teaming partners, clients, procurement contacts and potential job candidates. Consecutively, reinforce existing connections with points of contacts in your various social networking pipelines. Provide an "After Action Plan (AAP)" to achieve strategic response from the conference as follows:

- Create a follow-up plan to respond to everyone you spoke to at the conference.
- Complete a follow-up response on LinkedIn.
- Complete a follow-up response on Twitter.
- Complete a follow-up response on all of your Network Groups.
- Prepare and Share useful informational tips, links and information that are relevant to your conference outcome.
- Provide to others and you will receive value reactions to impact your relationship building.
- Always respond with a clear purpose in mind for connecting with your new potential contacts and have set goals for the relationships.
- Always measure your connection results of the conference to achieve great success at your next endeavor, but most importantly, measure cost versus benefit of attendance.

Make certain you set markers, goals and total purpose for the networking event. Make certain you understand your business and your purpose at the conference so you limit the chances of your competition gaining greater value. Keep in mind that some of your competitors are the best teaming partners. Think "Conference Competitive Intelligence (CCI)" in every effort of your conference presence.

Positioning for maximum Performance

There are numerous benefits to attending conference, breakout sessions, business luncheons and dinner events associated with conferences. The obvious is to listen to intelligent and knowledgeable speakers that provide presentations on important informational topics for useful business related areas of interest. You have to distinguish between the content of speakers that will align with your business. Sometimes speakers can bring valuable information, while some may deliver completely off the mark. So review the speakers and their content prior to the conference so that you are sure to attend the right session. Pay close attention to how the speaker gives their presentation and observe how the audience responds to the speaker. You might think the information isn't useful to you, but if the attendees are leaning forward, writing notes and holding up their phones and iPads to take pictures of the presentation slides, then the speaker is connecting with the audience. However, maybe the level of knowledge is less than what you need.

Most conferences provide an abundance of information that usually is not linked in a proper order for you to understand to relate to your business. Don't let bad conference content get in the way of getting the knowledge you need.

Listed below are a few techniques of positioning for maximum performance at a conference as follows:

- Provide a strategic and effective method and set of guidelines to conduct a successful "One-on-One" conference interview.
- Develop a "How to conduct a conference meeting" for a Before, During and After segment with evaluation
- Define what is actually provided at a Conference. Include the reality of the events that occurred and the How, Why, and When to go to a conference.

- Establish the Roles for going to a conference such as a "Prime," "Subcontractor," "Small Business" or potential teaming opportunity introduction.

Visit conferences by various levels of exposure (Observation, Market Branding/Marketing, Market Penetration, Networking by Pre-Planning and Pre-planning conference tactics/strategies.) (Politics)

Many businesses attend a multitude of conferences and hear the same comments from them such as:

- A lot of information, but no linkage to help my business.
- Great information, but what I do with it?
- It wasn't worth my time and money.
- It didn't have what I actually needed.
- The speakers didn't provide me with the right information.
- You hear the same thing from some of the same speakers at every conference.
- It doesn't help my small business.
- You only hear perspectives from large companies and federal agencies. This doesn't help my small business.
- Procurement agency or company representatives that are not decision makers.

LEVEL OF EXPOSURE: <u>OBSERVATION</u>

Prior to your visit to any conference, you want to prepare yourself with strategies of observation for the conference. You need to come up with some kind of strategic tactic of order. You have to make sure that you have defined your rules of engagement to the conference so that your observations will be meaningful.

<u>I have defined a three system, pre-optional, initial breakdown of the conference for preliminary observations as follows:</u>

- Pre-Opts—Always define a strategy of how you will view and interact in the conference:
  - ○ Know who you will approach at the conference.
  - ○ Gather prior intelligence of the targeted individuals, companies and agencies you plan to visit.
  - ○ Be mindful of your time to accomplish your mission for the conference.
  - ○ Don't over extend yourself in non-mission engagements of people.
  - ○ Don't focus your time on the marketplace myths of getting a procurement opportunity the day of the conference. Focus on introductions to future targeted conversations about procurement opportunities. These opportunities will be the ones that you have defined prior that an agency or business has to offer. It most likely will not be even mentioned at the conference. This illustrates that you did your homework/research about their organization.
- Day Operations—Task(s) to be completed throughout the entire day or days of the conference. Here are several ideas to implement throughout the day:
  - ○ Be on time for every scheduled event, breakout session and other appointments.

- o Do not meet with agencies or businesses for procurement opportunities until you are knowledgeable of that entity.
- o Follow your plan of action to ensure coverage of planned activities.
- o Provide a source of information, marketing materials, branding or other collateral that is unique to your targeted points of contact for the conference.
- Post-Opts
  - o Ensure you measure the success of the conference.
  - o Evaluate your mission completion of the conference.
  - o Follow-up with an email, mail out, social media source or other method of reply to all individuals you came in contact with throughout the conference.

LEVEL OF EXPOSURE: <u>BRANDING/MARKETING</u>

This is an important area of your business and a strategic positioning of your conference attendance. You should develop a branding or rebranding plan prior attending the conference.

<u>For your branding plan, you should identify or develop the following:</u>

- Develop your core organizational attributes.
- Conduct extensive internal, external and competitive research.
- Develop your structural and foundational innovative market positioning.

After you have developed your creative process, then you must proceed to the outlay:

- Branding appearance
- Branding guidelines
- Branding identity
- Graphics
- Naming
- Renaming
- Tagging development

After you develop the branding process, you must move to the brand positioning. You must create it to be relevant to the marketplace and it must be highly credible to everyone.

Some examples as follows:

- Apple and the iPhone
- Best Buy and Electronics
- BMW and the Ultimate Driving Machine
- Nike and Performance
- Operation Breakthrough and Breaking Business Barriers

You can adapt your own method of overall branding. We use a breakthrough method called "Operation Breakthrough Mapping" which is a process of identifying your business characteristics, analyzing the competitive brand alignment and position, reviewing and analyzing business opportunities to target an area that is unique to your product, solution or service and most of all, to appeal to your business audience.

MARKETING

After you have achieved your overall branding cycle, you should immediately move to the alignment of your marketing process. There are many marketing attributes to develop your business in today's fast changing technological times.

Here are a few ways to develop your marketing developmental process:

- Develop and understand your objectives.
- Know your precise target market.
- Know your competitors.
- What is the message you plan to transmit to your audience?
- What and Where is your audience?
- Mostly importantly, create your "Teaming Logic," or "OBT Strategic Teaming™," logic to perform your overall marketing plan of action.

The conferences you attend can be a great testing site for your marketing to see if it's positioned correctly or whether you are off the mark. You will encounter many other businesses, organizations and agencies. You can test your marketing strength by visiting with entities that you intend to never do business with to see if they find your marketing to be of great value or if it contains no content weight at all. You can compare your marketing collateral with other businesses of the same offerings or unrelated businesses. Never launch your marketing campaign at a conference if it is incomplete or not ready. Remember, a first impression is your lasting impression.

MARKETING PENETRATION

You have to create a strong, strategic marketing plan to achieve the greatest market penetration. You have to analyze all areas of your market and determine the paths to take your business to success. You should create a high level of interest for strong market penetration. You can accomplish this in many ways, but I will provide a few as follows:

- Conduct your research thoroughly on your solution, product or service offerings to fully identify a niche for market for penetration.
- Define an innovative and unique proposition to the market. For example, are you a Service Disabled Veteran Owned Small Business with a Facility Clearance, SKIFF or SCIF (Sensitive Compartmented Information Facility), etc.?
- Create a niche in the industry for your product, solution or service offering that allows a demand.

NETWORKING BY PRE-PLANNING

There are many benefits of planning ahead to truly fulfill your marketing goals for a conference attendance. You should conduct an extensive amount of due diligence based on the conference and the other business owners, exhibitors, teaming partners and professionals that will attend the conference. The due diligence should define an alignment of your business to their perspective businesses to reach a common marketing goal.

You should develop a "Networking Plan of Action (NPA)" to include the following, but not limited to:

* Check with your teaming partners to see if they are attending the conference and if so, see if they can support your marketing campaign for the conference.
* Schedule meetings with others within your network that will attend the conference to add value to your market penetration.
* Combine resources for the conference with your networking members to add more value to your marketing approach.

PRE-PLANNING CONFERENCE TACTICS AND STRATEGIES

The way to reach the different levels of exposure at the conference is to develop a set of marketing tactics and strategies to achieve the greatest impact of penetration. You should think technically at every level of the conference and create some type of logic for each day of the conference to reach your goals. Understanding that **Strategy** is the plan or method, whereas **Tactics** is the actions of doing.

Set of Marketing Tactics:

* Gathering conference data
* Performing due diligence on your market
* Executing your plans of action at the conference

Set of Marketing Strategies:

- Achieve 100% of marketing goals at conference.
- Meet with all the points of contacts you need to speak with at the conference to reach your marketing goals.
- Get your products, solutions or service offerings accepted by critical entities at the conference to receive a high level of interest.

POLITICS

The Political situation currently revolving around your business and the conference plays a huge part in what set of tactics you should employ while at a conference. You have to understand the political leadership level of the conference and how to achieve your marketing mission. The political impact to your business market may or may not affect your ability to accomplish your marketing penetration. You should stay neutral politically based on your own point of view, but be aware of the driving points at the conference setting. It is a very important part of the environment which you have to consider when penetrating the different levels of the conference agenda. Do your due diligence. Try to attend congressional meetings. Stay current on our countries' political views and world affairs that may impact your industry. Fully understand the economic situation for today, tomorrow and the future that surround your business marketplace and what effects it may have on the conference. This may impact your ability to implement various functions of your marketing tactics to accomplish your marketing strategies.

PART VI

STABILITY AND SUSTAINMENT TO SUCCESS!

IMPACT—IMPORTANCE OF PROTECTION!

SELF PROTECTION!

Chapter 8

The Non-Pursuit of getting Contracts and Credibility for Contracts

The secret of getting contracts

The Federal Government Contracting cycle has many traditional processes that are common throughout the marketplace, but comes at the expense of a very high percentage of business failures and low rates of success. Certain processes should be traditional in your entrepreneurial business processes; however, be very careful in the selection process. There are traditional processes that you should implement in your entrepreneurial track and also non-traditional processes such as:

Traditional Processes:

- Pursuit of marketplace certifications
- Contractor registration
- Business Insurance (Bonding when necessary)
- Training and education
- Attendance of Conferences, Symposiums, Seminars, etc. (Go with a purpose.)

Non-Traditional Processes:

- Certifications and Special Clearances that are not common (SKIF, Top Secret, etc.)
- Collaborated Strategic Partnership™ (CSP™)
- Teaming (OBT Strategic Teaming™)
- Strategic Marketing by Credibility™ (SMC™)
- Business Development by Credibility™ (BDC™)

Here are several reasons for the high percentages of business failures following traditional processes:

- Lack of marketplace knowledge
- Lack of industry knowledge
- Not doing the due diligence/homework
- Unaware of your market limitations
- Not understanding your product or services offerings for your targeted market
- Attending initial meetings for business development with Government agency representatives totally unprepared

The concept of obtaining contracts requires much greater work than merely accomplishing the traditional processes as listed above. It requires the entrepreneur/small business owner to deal with a much greater level of challenges. You should be innovative, creative, resourceful and adaptable to market challenges. In order to achieve contract success, you have to develop a source of unique, non-traditional processes. This process should be driven by the non-pursuit of attempting to get contracts. When you are going after contracts, you have to get ahead of the normal, traditional chase of contracts. You have to be strategic in your pursuit. You should actually think of innovative ways to place your business in the position of contract creation. What this means is planning ahead of your contract pursuit. You should research the solicitation that is structured in the forecast of an agency's procurement and define your business niche to alignment of that particular opportunity. Once you accomplished your knowledge capture of that solicitation or request for information (RFI,) then prepare a plan of pursuit around it. This is one of many examples of the "non-pursuit of getting contracts" that will provide you with less confusion in penetrating this complex contracting process.

You should develop a vetting process initially related to finding valuable organizations to obtain pre-observation of learning on the mere basics of government business. There are quite a few organizations for you to reach out to and by doing so, you will create a very solid business beginning. Some mentioned organizations that provide limited pre-business help or "starting your business" help are as follows:

- **MBDA** (Minority Business Development Associations)— MBDA advisors help minority business owners gain access to capital, contracts, market research and general business consulting. For more information go online to www.mbda.gov.
- **PTAC** (Procurement Technical Assistance Centers)— PTACs provide local, in-person counseling and training services for you, the small business owner. They are designed to provide technical assistance to businesses that want to sell products and services to federal, state, and/ or local governments. PTAC services are available either

free of charge, or at a nominal cost. PTACs are part of the Procurement Technical Assistance Program, which is administered by the Defense Logistics Agency.

- **SBA** (<u>Small Business Administration</u>)—Since its founding on July 30, 1953, the U.S. Small Business Administration has delivered millions of loans, loan guarantees, contracts, counseling sessions and other forms of assistance to small businesses. SBA provides assistance primarily through its four main functions:
  - o Access to Capital (Business Financing)
  - o Entrepreneurial Development (Education, Information, Technical Assistance & Training)
  - o Government Contracting (Federal Procurement)
  - o Advocacy (Voice for Small Business)
- **SBDC** (<u>Small Business Development Centers</u>)—SBDCs provide management assistance to current and prospective small business owners. SBDC services include financial counseling, marketing advice and management guidance. Some SBDCs provide specialized assistance with information technology, exporting or manufacturing. SBDCs are partnerships primarily between the government and colleges, administered by SBA. SBDC assistance is available virtually anywhere with 63 networks branching out with more than 900 delivery points throughout the U.S., the District of Columbia, Guam, Puerto Rico, American Samoa and the U.S. Virgin Islands. SBDC hosts include:
  - o 48 University-sponsored SBDC hosts: 16 SBDC locations are located at Historically Black Colleges and Universities. Two such Lead Centers are Howard

University in Washington, DC, and the University of the Virgin Islands, USVI.

o 8 Community college-sponsored SBDC hosts: Dallas-TX, UT, OR, NM, AZ, San Diego-CA, Los Angeles-CA and American Samoa

o 7 State-sponsored Lead SBDCs (CO, IL, IN, MN, MT, OH, & WV): *Since 1990, Congress has required all new Lead SBDCs be managed by institutions of higher education or women's business centers.*

For more information, go online to www.sba.gov/content/small-business-development-centers-sdbcs.

● **SCORE** (Service Corps of Retired Executives)—Non-profit association compromised of 13,000 plus volunteer business counselors throughout U.S. and its territories. SCORE members are dedicated to entrepreneur education and the formation, growth and success of small businesses nationwide. SCORE is a resource partner with the Small Business Administration. There is no fee for their services. For more information go online to www.sba.gov/content/score.

● **VBOC** (Veteran Business Outreach Centers)—VBOCs provide veterans with entrepreneurial development services such as business training, counseling and mentoring. The mission of the Veterans' Business Outreach Center (VBOC) is to help create, develop and retain veteran-owned small business enterprises. The VBOC provides entrepreneurial training through workshops and the Internet, counseling, technical assistance and resource utilization services to Veterans, Service-Disabled Veterans, Reservists, National Guard Members and Active Duty business owners and start-up entrepreneurs in the Southeast Region of the USA. This program is funded by the U.S. Small Business Administration to serve as a specialized agency of business and technical assistance for those veterans interested in starting or expanding a business. Before the VBOC can provide assistance, the Small Business Administration requires all clients to complete the Electronic Request for Counseling (ERFC) form. For more information go online to www.vboc.org.

- **WBC** (Women's Business Centers)—Women's Business Centers (WBCs) represent a national network of nearly 100 plus educational centers designed to assist women start and grow small businesses. WBCs operate with the mission to "level the playing field" for women entrepreneurs, who still face unique obstacles in the world of business. Through the management and technical assistance provided by the WBCs, entrepreneurs, especially women who are economically or socially disadvantaged, are offered comprehensive training and counseling on a variety of topics in many languages to help them start and grow their own businesses. For more information go online to www. sba.gov/content/women's-business-centers.

Remember that the organizations mentioned above are great resources to gather pre-business information and initial business developmental support. You have to reach out to other organizations to get you to the higher levels of business. Throughout your entire business cycle, keep in mind to achieve what others have done by the following examples:

Examples:

- The Military doesn't go to battle without a "Mission Plan."
- Professional Athletes/Coaches do not play the game without a "Game Plan."
- An Architect will not authorize the design/construction of a building without design drawings/plans.

So why do most Business Owners/Entrepreneurs go into business without designing a Structure, a Team, a Business Plan and a host of other action plans? Why do they proceed without business plan/ roadmaps, developing processes, methodologies, structure and strategies?

Business is like a host of regular season games that lead to the ultimate championship. During the preseason, you prepare, practice, work out, do due diligence. You create a winning game plan and pick a winning team. You build strategies and commit to a dedicated practice regimen through hard work and intensity. Overall, you attempt to accomplish all of this to get to one championship game to win. If you slack in any of the areas, don't fully develop the internal systems or take a short cut, you will see the end results which may not be favorable to your advantage. This is the same with developing your business, if you take shortcuts, don't fully research your industry, merely don't complete what is needed, then your business will fail or settle to a level not of your choosing which will be below your high level of standards.

Time Management to Value Positioning

Remember that during your pursuit of contracts, you should not count on finding your opportunities merely by viewing of www. fedbizopps.gov. You should get ahead of the contract opportunities by speaking with Government procurement representatives about opportunities and solicitations that have not been published in the public publications or boards. You should locate opportunities listed in the procurement forecast of various agencies either classified as a RFI or inquiry. If you are gathering opportunities from the databases that are already posted such as RFPs (Request for Proposals,) then you are too late, meaning you have lost that opportunity prior to even writing the proposal.

Every step you take in your business should be measured for its accomplishment or failure characteristics. Re-examine and then implement the best results. This can be repeated as best practices to maximize your time management. When you proceed through every step of your business, you should have a plan of action or strategy to make certain you are always moving forward to achieve the greatest value proposition for your business.

We were able to measure our ability to achieve success by the example of our business model, business plan, strategic model, marketing model, branding model, implementation model and execution model by being chosen by the number one ranking financial credit card company in the world as a Success Story—small business owner/entrepreneur as a success in the Government Contracting Marketplace. This is a true reality of success to measure from when developing and conducting business. Another example is being able to break all barriers to attract the Number #1 ranking and largest Government Contractor in Federal Government Contracting as the Major Sponsor to our business to attempt to reach small businesses all around the country to teach them how to do business with the Federal Government in Contracting.

We have even attracted the Department of Defense (DOD-DLA), US Navy, US Air Force, Tuskegee Airmen and other large companies to illustrate an interest in our processes by means of participating as speakers at our formal workshops. This is an ultimate, maximum result of success by any means of measuring success. To be validated in some form of success by these significant class successors is Value Positioning at its best!

Positioning for procurement

In recent years, contracts have become limited to small businesses of all types, especially minority businesses, service-disabled, veteran-owned small businesses and women-owned small businesses because there appears to be a limited number of qualified small businesses of these entities This situation presents itself because most small businesses (Service-Disabled Veteran-Owned, Women-Owned) find themselves not contract-ready even though they assume they are ready.

Most small businesses are not positioned for procurement for the following reasons, not exclusively:

- They do not have their businesses equipped with the proper certifications.

- They do not have their business structure defined.
- They do not have their team built for business.
- They lack industry knowledge.
- They do not have their financials in order or finances to operate the contract.
- Various other reasons that limit their abilities to be ready for procurement pursuit

In the branding and marketing stages of your business, you have to widen your approach so that you are highly recognized in the industry and the best way to do this is by credibility of others. Less than 1% of small businesses understand this method of "Teaming" or our process "OBT Strategic Teaming." Most small businesses that fail normally never get to the point of developing a true teaming collaboration or they team with the wrong people which led them down a road to destruction.

There are many ways to accomplish proper positioning for procurement, but I will list several successful ones as follows:

- Develop an Innovative Team Approach™ (ITA™)
- Develop a Strategic Credibility Program™ (SCP™)
- Develop a Forecasting Method of Approach™ (FMA™)

Remember, your positioning should have a minimum alignment of the following:

- Advisors
- Advisory Board Members
- Associates

- Businesses (outside of your business)
- Contractors
- Demographics
- Employees
- Family
- Geographical locations
- Legacies
- Legal Supporters
- Liaisons
- Marketing
- Mentors
- Observation Connected Mentors
- Political Leaders
- Primes-to-Partners
- Protégés
- Resources
- Subcontractors
- Teaming Partners

The Art of OBTS—STRATEGIC TEAMING

TEAMING: It is so awesome to build a home with a solid foundation that can withstand a serious storm. It is the same with building your business, always first and foremost build your business foundation to withstand the most unexpected experiences. Build your structure, ensure alignment at every step, set your perimeters, create an interlinking cross structure of business, establish a collaborated resource exchange and build growth together. This is all high-level language of business with a tremendous amount of detail at every angle of the business. Credibility by means of teaming will introduce you to the most sophisticated means for doing business. I have designed and adopted this method throughout my entire military, civilian and business career. From a local to regional to national to global standpoint, this method has been proven to be very successful. Most Small Business Owners/Entrepreneurs think that they have to develop their business on their own and this is not the way to do it. Remember, as mentioned earlier in this Chapter, a lot of times you have to be creative, innovative and follow non-traditional methods to accomplish success and this is one of those times. Even though this is considered non-traditional, it should be traditionally used by all Small Business Owners/Entrepreneurs doing business now and in the future.

My method, "OBTS Teaming™ or OBT Strategic Teaming™," is so effective, widely needed and requested by many small businesses and even large businesses, that I am launching a book series of "Teaming," "Entrepreneurship" and "Career" developmental tools and processes to reach the many National to Global Small Business Owners/Entrepreneurs and even various large businesses.

Prepare your business with the resources to withstand any storm that may consist of business adversities, obstacles and struggles. Of course, we can't prepare for everything, but we can prepare to be better equipped than the 82% plus businesses that go out of business between the first and second year of their business journey. Always prepare for longevity, not short-term wealth and your business future will be long-lasting and sustainable.

<u>Here is a brief list of important factors that we use in our Art of OBTS Teaming or OBT Strategic Teaming Model:</u>

- We develop our business model, concepts and processes in collaboration with others of the same business alignment.
- We build our business foundation, structure, team, support structure, solutions, products, service offerings and all other processes with total interlinking connections that generate growth building.
- We build mutual relationships that have reciprocating interchange of resources.
- We only perform business with others that have same business characteristics and personal traits of our entire team.
- We develop a three-level, minimum internal and external business operating structure that creates a "Three Check System" (TCS) to validate every step of our business process.

When constructing your business processes, always design them with measuring mechanisms, validation tools, evaluation factoring, business layer leveraging, business connectivity, system and structure alignment and mutual developmental growth, etc.

Our "OBT Strategic Teaming™" system collaborates with team members at every aspect of our business structure internally and externally. We design our entire business cycle with experts of proven personal, business and procurement experiences and track records. We suggest you do the same in your entrepreneurial journey.

Our Art of OBTS™—Strategic Teaming provides quite a lot of resources. The outcome of our strategic teaming creates an astonishing, unlimited amount of innovative resources. The benefit of strategic teaming is that it provides more resources than mentoring, although mentoring is part of our strategic teaming process. I will list a few so that you have an idea of the great benefits that develop from a "True Teaming" as follows:

- Added Value Propositions
- Branding
- Business Development
- Contracts
- Credibility
- Funding
- Marketing
- Ownership
- Partnerships
- Relationships
- Resources
- Solutions
- Structural Strength
- Many other innovative resources

Chapter 9

The Circle of Refinement

Business has a revolving cycle that generates a need to improve it constantly. You should always generate new and innovative ways to control your circle of reliable business associates and business affiliated individuals that will impact your business towards success. During your business cycle, you should always surround yourself with people that have more knowledge than you so that you constantly build a greater business cycle.

Creation of Support (Mentorship/Protégé)

Traditionally, all Small Business Owners/Entrepreneurs search continuously on a direct or indirect path for mentors and some never find a single one. In a blink of an eye, I realized that my logic of **"OBT Strategic Teaming™"** had already created all the mentors I needed plus more. This illustrates another measure of a successful business process. As I developed my teaming structure, I had accumulated quite a bit of mentors directly and indirectly, not purposely across an entire business spectrum in many concentrated areas.

To name a few concentrated areas as follows:

- Business Development
- Contract Procurement Pursuit
- Procurement Education and Training
- Procurement understanding
- Business Observation
- Business Awareness
- Business Structure
- Business Support
- Resource Support
- Financial Support
- Marketplace Segmentation targeting
- Many other concentrated areas

Ironically, by the creation of my strategic teaming logic, it defined and produced a source of unlimited mentorships in many ways as such:

- either by large company C-level personnel
- large business unofficial mentor—protégé arrangements within the teaming arrangements
- company-to-company mentor protégé relationships
- advisory board development without a single request—all advisory board members had a high interest to be involved with our growth.

When I evaluated my business model pertaining to the results of mentorship through my critical teaming model, I quickly realized that the planning and preparation through my teaming relationships would produce all the mentorships I needed. In addition, I designed my teaming model to produce an Advisory Board having direct alignment with my business model and indirect paths to capture the business unknowns. Below is an example of the structure of my Advisory Board that produces a tremendous amount of benefits:

- Prior or current CEOs of Fortune 100, 500, 1000 businesses
- Attorneys (Actually Senior Partners of Law Firms)
- Financial Firms (CPAs, Senior Investors, etc.)
- High Ranking Officials
- Former Political Officials
- Technology Experts
- Former Public Agency Directorates

Through my "OBT Strategic Teaming™" logic, I discovered a wealth of knowledge transfer that provided a great resource for mentoring indirectly to a direct means. I had spoken with a CEO at a Top Fortune 100 (Number #1 four years ago) Large Engineering/Construction Company, which is a Subcontractor, and he told me that I didn't need him as a Mentor since I had mentors from all aspects of business by having some of the largest businesses in the United States as Subcontractors and C-Level support of mentorship from all of them including him.

Here are a few examples:

- Pastor Ricky Tevada: Faith-driven Business Support and mentorship support. What you learn in church can definitely help you in many ways personally and in business. Just listen and observe. As a Pastor, Leader and Friend, he is always in an observational mindset, so he sees business situations, listens and counsels many businesspeople. A Pastor can set you up literally with unlimited resources even when it is not intentionally set up that way.

- Dr. Marilyn Gowing: Met with her as a Senior Vice President of the Number #1 Fortune 100 Company in Risk Management/Human Capital Solutions that became my Subcontractor. She was the prior Director of the U.S. Office of Personnel Management and prior Senior Consultant for a company that developed the Training/Assessment for the Iraq Police Force. She became my Advisory Board Member, Friend, Networking Support and a strong mentorship support.

- Monica Coney: Met with her in conjunction as a Sales Manager for Dr. Gowing and soon became a tremendous support for unlimited, strategic networking connections and business resources.

- Attorney Ray Jackson: In 2003, Tom Delay—Majority Leader of the U.S. House of Representatives appointed Ray Jackson as honorary co-chairman of the Business Advisory Council. In 2006, D Magazine—"Ray Jackson named one of Americas Premier Lawyers". In 2007, D Magazine—"Ray Jackson named one of the Best Lawyers in Dallas". In 2008, Eclipse Magazine—"Ray Jackson named one of Dallas' Dynamic Lawyers". As a man of the highest integrity and strong intellect, he has played a vital role in my success and future. Ray not only provides the utmost of excellence for legal services, but provides the highest quality of business foresight and a path of absolute strong mentorship towards spiritual belief and business intelligence. Ray's staff (Partner—Attorney Kobby T. Warren, Cristal, Associate—Ms. Charles) provides the utmost customer service and illustrates the excellence of what a staff should be like in any industry.

- Dr. David Morris, Ph.D., J.D.: President and CEO of a Consulting company that developed the Training/ Assessment and revived the Iraq Police Force. His company became my Subcontractor and he became an Advisory Board Member for my company. Introduction by Dr. Marilyn Gowing.

- Roger McMillin, Retired Chief Judge of the Mississippi Court of Appeals: Partner of Consulting Firm of David Morris, Ph.D., J.D. and Advisory Board Member for my company. Introduction by Dr. Marilyn Gowing.

- Jenny Vallner, Director of Sales of one of the largest Telecommunications companies in the world. Jenny and I formed a "Teaming" relationship between our companies at the beginning of my business launch. Jenny saw the vision and importance of Teaming to accomplish greater success. Jenny's company became the first largest of my "Teaming Partners" of my 1000 plus teaming partners today. They have been the central core of my success.

- Howard Ady, Vice President of a large firm of 69,000 professionals in 40 countries across the Americas, Europe and Asia Pacific that provide end-to-end IT and business process services that facilitate the ongoing evolution of clients' businesses. Howard and I formed a business relationship when several years ago he was a Corporate Vice President of a company that had over 20,000 plus professionals. Howard provided total "Teaming Partnership" and "Mentoring" at the highest levels of Entrepreneurial Business Solutions. Howard's prior company went through a merger of combined companies from 20,000 to 69,000 plus employees which without hesitation strengthen our "Teaming" efforts by supporting our organization further with even greater support and resources. Howard is a man of the greatest integrity, strategic mindset and intellect. A great personable and business friend.

- James T. George, CEO & Founder, USAR, Retired Colonel and Norris Middleton, COO, USAR, Retired Lieutenant Colonel and staff became one of my vital Teaming Partners. Norris and James provided me great mentorship in business, entrepreneurial vision and an intellectual foresight of teaming.

- Robert Sessom, Minister of Wisdom and Friend (Over 33 years): No matter what the circumstances, he would always provide positive advice, business support, faith support and spiritual strength at the highest levels as it relates to all areas of business and personal affairs. One of the world's most talented professionals in Art, Graphics, Music and Spiritual Development.

- Don Carter: Prayer support and mentoring through Faith support. Introduction to other associated business partners, organizations and business intelligence discussions at C-Levels.

- Dennis Green, Colonel, USAF, Retired: Advisory Board Member, fellow Military Counterpart, Faith and business support at the highest levels. Support in networking, speaking engagement support, introduction to Tuskegee Airmen and networking and relationship support.

Introduction from Robert Sessom above. Also by support of Ronald Graves, Colonel, USAF, Retired; LTC. Robert Campbell PhD. and Brigadier General Wayne Wright, USAF—Advisory Board Members.

- Danny Lovelady, LTC, USAR, Retired: One of my C-Level Executives, Advisory Board Member, Friend, fellow Military Counterpart, Faith and Business Support.

- Wayne Wright, Brigadier General, USAF: Advisory Board Member, fellow Military Counterpart, Faith and business support at the highest levels.

- Danny Portee, USAR, Retired, CEO/President of PME: Our business support relationship and friendship was generated through Danny reaching out to me for support to build his business and now has achieved great success. I provided protégé support and soon after networking support from Danny, also introduction of key professionals and companies for network interchange from him as well. Fellow Military Counterpart, Faith and business support at the highest levels.

- Reginald Johnson, University of North Texas, one of the top universities in our nation. Reginald and I joined ranks as "Teaming Partners" at the beginnings of my business vision. Reginald has a great intellect of "business-to-university" teaming arrangements. Reginald has supported both of my companies and has been a great resource of true partnership and friendship. Reginald's university is one of the largest Veteran support universities in our nation. This plays a vital role in our Teaming relationship and for the future of my fellow Veterans.

* There are hundreds more that played a central role of mentoring me! I could write a book just on "Mentorship by Teaming™ (MBT™.)" What's ironic is that all of the thousands of support members were introduced through a series of parallel relationships either in business, friendship, networking and definitely trusted and reliable sources in alignment of each other.

You have to balance your mentorship to protégé relationships whether direct, indirect, official or unofficial in order to capture your overall business' strategic alignment both internally and externally.

Building layers of strategic support protection

Your creation of support in business should come from many entities such as your spouse, significant other, family member, friend, peer or any support type person that will help you to stay motivated or just merely be a sounding support for you. A great support structure of individuals and/or groups can add value to you as a Small Business Owner/Entrepreneur because their perspective is seen from the outside of your business which can create a positive strategy that may not be seen from an internal standpoint. They can provide a clear view sometimes of your business performance, your good and bad approaches of people and sometimes even your good and bad business practices. Just be willing to listen and observe their reactions to your actions.

As a Small Business Owner/Entrepreneur, you have to really research to creatively understand the connectivity of the business process—procurement contracting and the overall way of doing business in the Federal Government. There are absolutely no realistic industry standards of business practices to help you in your entrepreneurial journey. Conferences do not cover these areas of concentration even though it states "How to do business with the Federal Government" or "Understanding the Procurement in Federal/Public Sector Government Contracting" or "Procurement Contracts are won at Conferences." There are many more slogans to entice attendance of the Small Business Owner/Entrepreneur. The results are frustration and eventually failure of small businesses because they rely on these slogans to gain the knowledge to do business and this is a problem. It is the Small Business Owner/ Entrepreneur's responsibility to gain an understanding of this complex and confusing system of doing business in Federal Government Contracting. One of my recommendations is to create a support, knowledge group or some type of "Knowledge Support Structure (KSS)" to help you in your business endeavors. A lot of your conferences, seminars and other events hosted by Government Agencies speak about general topics related to doing business with the Government, but it is either segmented, disconnected from business understanding or merely reflects a great lack of knowledge beyond the 101-type lecture. One of the major problems of most conferences is the lack of small business perspective teachings. In order to reach a certain level of your audience, you have to obtain the speakers that can relate to their business levels by experience. But as a Small Business Owner/Entrepreneur, you have to prep ahead of your attendance to the conferences with a plan of action to capture what you particularly need from the conference. Don't go with the idea that you are going to capture a procurement contract, go with a real purpose. Again, this is where your support structure, advisors, knowledge support groups, etc. can help you from an external standpoint. Scout conferences, seminars and other events to understand what support you can really leverage from them. Remember the important key concepts to capture knowledge at a conference as follows:

- Analyze
- Evaluate
- Listen
- Observe
- Purpose Driven Missions
- Technical & Tactical Approach

Support limitations

There is such a thing as too much support or getting the wrong support. This is where you need to be very cautious in your planning for support. You need to understand your surroundings when dealing with people. You need to know their limit of supporting you. You definitely need to be able to determine whether or not the support is advantageous or disadvantageous prior to obtaining it. As a successful Small Business Owner/ Entrepreneur, I have experienced the transitions of people during great times, not the best of times and the bad times. I have watched and experienced different types of people that gravitate when times are great, you can't shake them, but when times are neutral or there's a hint that things may not be going so well, they shrink away like a passing storm. Some people have positive attributes no matter what the circumstances may be and some are just merely negative and become a total hindrance.

BUSINESS PRACTICES

Based on business practices I have observes, there are many different types and what I see more than I want to see is "cut-throat" business practices. We always think that the environment of Corporate America harvests these types of bad practices and we say we will leave that bad business pattern out of our Entrepreneurial journeys, but a lot of Entrepreneurs add them right back into their business culture. This happens especially when money (large amounts) approaches, potential of valuable contract winnings and when the vision of business success arrives. Always deal with others that are grounded by loyalty, trust and their ability to be seen as helpers to others.

Development of a multi-layer, multi-step interlinking Team

You should thrive to achieve "Support by Collaboration (SBC.)" Collectively, things can be accomplished in business faster and in a more protected manner if you position yourself with the right supporters. This is really exciting because "OBT Strategic Teaming™" is the ultimate and most perfected way of creating such a great support structure by combing resources and staging a high collaboration with others. There are so many rewards in this phase of methodology. It is truly underutilized by so many Small Business Owners/Entrepreneurs. Less than 1% of businesses fully operate in the manner of strategic teaming. You should make certain you totally collaborate to the maximum abilities of your support relationships. When you develop your strategic team of support, you should create multiple layers of teams that align in horizontal and vertical knowledge base modeling along with multiple building structures from the beginning of your business to the level of success. There should be a total interconnection at every point of your business, internally and externally. Your support growth surroundings calculation standpoint example:

		Strategic Logic +Teaming +Structure + Support		
SUPPORT	=	OBSERVATION *Long-term Planning by Strategies*	/	*Bad Situations, Support by Failure*
		Surroundings +Marketing + Business Development + Growth, Trust, Loyalty		

Limitations of Awareness

A Small Business Owner/Entrepreneur's approach throughout his or her business journey should rely on attention to detail of the business environment and their surrounding support system. You should create a system based on your support limitations by means of vision markers at every step of your business progress. You should provide an internal and external awareness strategy of screening your business associates, affiliates and any one that may have an impact on your business.

You should effectively create a "Screening Support Awareness Program (SSAP)" solely to measure, analyze, check and approve any support of individuals or companies you may do business with currently and in the future. From experience, even having dealt with people to assess and validate their support intentions in a form of Human Capital Solutions, I have had to really create a detail support screening system.

Listed below are several limitations of awareness validation methods for screening support:

- Observe how that potential support member treats his or her spouse or significant other during non-business hours.
- Observe how that potential support member acts under pressure.
- Discuss a potential large dollar amount contract that you may or may not potentially win to check the grounding factor of that potential support member which I define as "Internal Personal Value—IPV."

Listed below are several limitations of awareness indicators for screening support:

- Business observation
- Business representation
- Character representation
- Personality trait
- Value proposition

Economic Awareness: You should know the limitations of your economic awareness because as a Small Business Owner/ Entrepreneur the economic environment can impact your business to the point of immediate failure or feats of great success. Complete your due diligence, stay current with the country's economic situation and globally if you are attempting to perform international business and maintain your familiarity with the political persuasion.

Expectations: Never set false expectations of success. Your expectations usually do not meet your primary goal setting and when you have others involved in your business affairs, they need to be very patient people. If they are head-strong as to time urgency, get—rich-quick oriented, then you should leave that type person out of your business affairs.

Vultures/Bad Influences: Keep yourself away from vultures, in other words, people that just want what you have to benefit only them. These types of individuals are the ones that will take from you what you don't have bolted down. They will steal your ideas, methodologies, logic, processes and immediately try to benefit from them in the public eye. They will approach you with the friendliest and most sincere initial support without you having to ask. Always keep them in the outer layer of your business with protective measures in place. Never let an un-vetted potential support member, business associate or affiliate know about your internal sources (methodologies, approaches, processes, procedures, strategies) of your business.

Be aware of people wanting to team with you immediately without wanting to sign a legal agreement of the arrangements. Never place yourself into a teaming situation that is not properly vetted. For example: Never place yourself into a database of other businesses to team with just anybody that has opportunities. Never think that teaming is just merely two companies working together without a vetted and mutual relationship of understanding. Cultivate your relationships in a teaming arrangement to ensure trust, loyalty and total collaboration. Don't just signup to a database where there are posted opportunities, form teaming arrangements without limits so each party can truly benefit and just to make money together. This is the true meaning of "Teaming". Don't make the mistake of many!

Trust Circle

Building a Circle of Trust in Business: Building a Trust Circle requires a great deal of focus fostering on collaborative teamwork, continuous integrity, dedicated loyalty and certitude between each other. Each person within the closed and protected circle should accept shared responsibility of trust among everyone else in the circle no matter what circumstances may arise. The area of focusing on shared responsibilities normally will eliminate individuals from the circle because if any one of the individuals is about themselves only, then they will not accept shared responsibility of any kind.

Some of the highest qualities that are required by individuals in a circle of trust are as follows:

- Faith
- Acceptance
- Assurance
- Certainty
- Certitude
- Conviction
- Loyalty
- Fidelity
- Sureness
- Credibility
- Dependence

- Reliance
- Persistence to Trust

Always try to "Fast Track" individuals that seek entry into your circle of trust by the means of their "values." This is extremely important because the bond of your trust cycle has to align with the highest integrity of self-driven values. Do not compromise in any aspect of this area. "It is truly common by experience that the trust and character of individuals align with the integrity of all individuals' commonality will be of the same value." People of trust similarity will share a great deal of parallelism and resemblance in their demeanor. Always look at those traits as an early indicator of good values.

Always thoroughly evaluate to gain clarity of your surroundings when people attempt to seek entry into your circle of trust.

Building Trust focuses on the relationship between trust, leadership and collaboration. A key interest of high trust is driven more by aligned commitment and shared responsibility than by an assessment of individual capabilities and values.

Shared Responsibility: Shared responsibility lies at the heart of any effective teaming collaboration. When individuals and teams work together well, their mutually held responsibility provides the basis for the strategic connection. When you want to create shared responsibility, you need to focus your sole attention in the following areas:

- Collaborative Attitudes
- Common Values

- Mutual Personal and Business Commitments
- Strategic Thinking
- Tenacity to Succeed with Integrity at all Aspects of Business
- Trust Building

Collaborative Attitude: Collaborative attitude starts with a commitment of involving others. This commitment can have various motivations within the scope of business. Involvement can bring together diverse points of view and lead to a better outcome of trust and the ability to build a stronger bond together. With involvement, there comes a sense of shared ownership and a high level of energy for implementation among your team members. Involving others also provides an opportunity to influence their views and build a strong, undivided coalition. Ideally, a collaborative attitude is also motivated by a desire to benefit through other points of view and to be influenced as well as build a circle of trust that has no break points.

Common Values: Common values are defined by the same beliefs and mindsets of individuals that share a common concept of trust and loyalty. These values contribute to the overall circle of trust to maximize results with no fail points, with values such as innovation, motivation and common courtesy passing through the business from each member of the circle of trust.

Mutual Personal and Business Commitments: Mutual personal and business commitments are of the same values in a circle of trust. There is no separation in the quality measure of two or more individuals within the determination of building a long-lasting relationship of obligation among each other. The formulation measures the internal and external strength of the relationship and all measures of trust are equal to each other no matter who gains at various points of the business.

Strategic Thinking: Strategy is about recognizing and making various decisions and choices. In the service of collaboration and shared responsibility, strategic thinking involves choosing who to involve in your business, how they will be involved, what the level of involvement will be and how the group will work together in all aspects of business collectively. Involving individuals in decisions that affect them is a solid demonstration of respect. Establishing direction collaboratively through explicit and solid agreements ensures the group is aligned and able to work together. Recognition of this alignment reinforces mutual trust in the entire circle or groups within the circle of trust.

Tenacity to Succeed with Integrity at all Aspects of Business: Throughout the entire business cycle, having the ability and perseverance to reach mutual success with the highest level of values to achieve a common goal in all business areas is a true necessity.

Secondary Structured Layers of Trust: When constructing your circle of trust, you should develop an internal and external layer by secondary trusted members that are truly vetted even if they are family members or loved ones such as your spouse, true friends, your Pastor or Advisory Board Members so that additional shield of trust and protection can be formed from a secondary standpoint. By experience, the reason for this is because people can turn on you in a blink of an eye and most times the intent was never to support you from the beginning, it was just to feed off your knowledge or to attempt to take your valuable strategies, ideas or business.

Leverage Money for the sake of your Success: A lot of times, people leverage money through their business with a need to feed off your success. You have to be extremely careful with the idea of borrowing from someone that has not been vetted into your circle of trust. Remember, I mentioned the "values" earlier that were extremely important. These attributes will appear very quickly in difficult times to illustrate that the values of all are not common and this can create a business nightmare. In other words, do not take any resources from anyone unless every aspect of your circle of trust has been validated for that particular individual.

Trusted Helpers in Business: By experience, I have accumulated many trusted supporters for my business journey. I have observed, reviewed, measured, analyzed and evaluated by trial methodology and validated all business aspects to ensure true helpers and supporters. This allowed my circle of trust to define itself to be a very solid structure of business resources. However, nothing is full-proof, so I want to help you to maintain all of your check points of trust no matter how long it may take so that you do not lose the integrity of your circle of trust. We are all human and humans make mistakes, wrong judgment calls and many times jump to end solutions without all of the facts to sustain the reality.

People that turned the Trust into Uncertainty: Don't think that people who turn on you are always people that you don't know; people that you have only known a short time can do the same. You can get blind-sided with totally unexpected surprises in business. Constant communication is the key to eliminating false accusations and counterproductive results of trust. But the ultimate circle of trust relies on "Trust" and some people just merely go with the persuasion of others without checking facts. True friends, true committed circle of trust members, will validate all information before accepting the mistaken judgment of others. This is a costly experience and will lead to ruined relationships. Time is a defining measure of great things, but in business, time can be a sign of failure, disappointment and a misled sourcing tool. It is extremely important that people are certain through their perspective of understanding that business can be thrown off by many obstacles and adversities. This is why you have to fully understand that patience has to be built into the trust of others and when things turn negative, you have to maintain your trust of the circle. People can only provide what they can and most times, it is only trust. Everything else is here today and maybe gone tomorrow in business, except trust is still rooted at the core, personal and business related.

Selection of people who you let in your "circle of affiliation" can minimize, impact or accelerate your abilities to achieve success.

You have to be very selective as to who you affiliate with as friends and even more strategic when it comes to business. In a friendship, you can agree to disagree and still be able to live with or without this person. In a friendship, you can continue to disagree on many areas and still cultivate your relationship. Friendships are built on the elements of trust, integrity, loyalty and willingness to do for each other without receiving benefits.

It is easier when as an entrepreneur/small business owner can depend on support from their friends. It becomes slightly more difficult when you have support from friends that cannot relate to you in business or if they choose to be negative about your business venture. It is important for you to understand that you should not allow any negativity into your business journey. Some people will never understand the process of business and that is ok. Things become more complicated when you let people get involved in your business that are not friends and they are negative thinking individuals. What you have to understand is that no matter what people think, you have to maintain your ability to achieve success.

Your business can be greatly hindered by people if you provide them with enough information to do damage against your pathway to success. You have to be very cautious when speaking with people about your business. Never provide them information and details of your intricate secrets, patents or the process flow of your business because some people will steal your ideas and take away your ability to achieve success. Further in the book, I will provide more detail as to how people can either help you in your business journey or how they can totally disrupt your business.

Selection of the right people to involve in your business can accelerate your ability to achieve success for your business journey. In Chapter 9 of the book, I will provide more detail on the alignment and important characteristics of the "Circle of Affiliation (COA,)" but listed below are a few important factors to consider on people selection:

* Make certain they have true, positive values of character.
* Make certain they possess the greatest integrity.
* Make certain they share equal responsibility of trust in your business.

- Make certain that their personal values are of the highest standards.
- Make certain that you research and define the person's business knowledge.

In your selection of people, make certain you know their motives and mission towards their scope of business. You want to be certain they have your best interest in mind aligned with their business. Don't collaborate with one-track, one-way professionals with their own agendas.

Surround yourself with people that can generate support, knowledge and wealth of information.

It is important for you to place yourself in a direct, but more effectively, in an indirect presence of experienced and professional, knowledgeable type individuals or groups. My experience in this area has been tested time-and-time again over my life. I can go back as early as my childhood. Throughout my childhood and up to college, I attached myself to peers that seemed to have retained more knowledge than I had. I saw this as a plus for my growth and development to Entrepreneurship. I observed my peer's parents that seemed to set the presence of true role models looking into the future to implement ideas for me.

During the period of my private sector career couple with my military career, I had an opportunity to work and manage various collaborated projects with various top fortune 100—500 large companies, medium and small businesses, U.S. Department of Defense, Independent Government Agencies, non-profit and for-profit organizations, universities, U.S. Political Officials and 23 Allied Countries' representatives. I took advantage of learning a great deal of knowledge from these individuals and the high-level military officials and executive management professionals that I directly or indirectly supported.

You should always try to position yourself and your team around others that have proven careers and business successes. Make certain that these professionals align with your business scope directly or indirectly and innovatively and strategically align with your entire business. Imagine you and your team members are on a football field and you know that there are 100 yards of field to cover from goal-to-goal and you have to make a touchdown. You gather 11 team members that possess a certain amount of knowledge, skills and a high level of trust among each other to drive to the goal to reach one common goal—success. You analyze and measure the opposition, the motivation of the members, the audience, the referees and the opposition's Coaches (Leaders) as to their demeanor. In other words, you not only include your team members around you with great knowledge, but you observe everyone in your perspective surroundings and learn from them play-by-play.

You have to retain knowledge from all the people you surround yourself with and retain unwanted information from people that will be around you, not just to measure knowledge capture.

You should attend various events, seminars, conferences and symposiums just to gather knowledge capture and to build your "Circle of Knowledge (COK)" as we call it. I will discuss in greater detail about innovative ways to maximize your knowledge at conferences, events, seminars and symposiums in Chapter 7 of this book.

Don't align yourself with fast, get-rich-quick and impatient people.

There are many types of people in the world of business and entrepreneurship that can impact your business success in a positive or negative way.

One great indicator is never go into business with people that are fast talking in thinking, wanting to gain "get-quick" results from the business and very impatient about receiving monetary gain of profits from the business. Imagine a business partner, investor or partial owner that wants and demands quick monetary results, fast return on investment and just extremely impatient. This causes total chaos and tends to lead to business failure.

Here are some great indicators to keep in mind when you expose yourself to new individuals and even people you have known for a while:

- Indicator 1—Carefully observe people that speak fast and laugh loud when having a conversation with them. They may be covering up negative motives against you.
- Indicator 2—Observe the level of conversation when they speak. A lot of times they speak loud and fast about a subject matter to cover the lack of knowledge about that subject.
- Indicator 3—As you listen to people's conversation about business and they keep mentioning about getting rich fast,

this is a definite sign for you to keep some distance from these individuals. We all would like to get rich quick in business, but patience is the best virtue.

- Indicator 4—Listen between the lines because if you observe a get-rich-quick type thinking individual, gradually you will hear the negative concepts of business.
- Indicator 5—Entrepreneurship is a tremendous challenge and takes a great deal of patience. Impatience can be a great defilement to an entrepreneur's success. Don't get caught up with impatient people especially when they take part in your business.

Every segment of your relationships as it pertains to your business should maintain high levels of patience, agility, flexibility, tenacity and determination with balance and "Strategic Slow Overlapping Observation (SSOO.)"

Recap, Re-Build and always re-evaluate your Circle

Recap, as a reminder, always continuously, thoroughly and constantly pursue the clarity of your surroundings of people in your "Circle of Trust (COT)" to ensure complete close proximity of near accurate, full-scope trust as much as humanly possible.

Never assume that trust is the central and main focus of your trusted members. Absolutely maintain open communication related to all aspects of trust, loyalty and support.

<u>Always keep the following items of interest at the top of your priority of trust as follows:</u>

- Ability to cope with Change
- Ability to do for others more than Self
- Attitude
- Expectations
- Grounded or ungrounded
- Limitations
- Loyalty
- Observations
- Respectful
- Short-fused or Long-fused Mind Set
- Support
- Teaming mindset
- Unity
- Values

Chapter 10

The Ring of Protection

It is very important in your initial business planning developmental cycle to design a protection, security and safety net to ensure you and your business is secure in day-to-day operations. This protection should defend you, all C-level professionals of your organization and every aspect of your business and its successes. By using strategic teaming measures, you can achieve many areas of protection that can extend through the cycle of your business and your personal security as well. Through experience, I have dealt with quite a bit of inside and outside attempts to penetrate my business processes, methodologies, innovations and overall business. During my entire military career, we extensively train to be able to protect our Nation against foreign enemies. In business, you have to train, train and train even more to protect your business interest and yourself from domestic opposition. In order to accomplish this mission of protection for all measures of your business, you have to create layers of security and protection to provide a totally safe business environment.

Here are some of the layers of security and protection:

- Maintain trusted advisors.
- Generate trusted teaming relationships.
- Don't trust anyone in business until trust is proven or earned.
- Design trusted measuring methods to keep balance of truth between all partners.
- Make certain all agreements are completed by legal documents and by an Attorney.
- Don't assume that trust exists in a business relationship—implant it every time.
- Even though you have legal agreements, always continue to assess the bond of trust.
- Limitations of business information are set by the level of trust.
- Don't govern your business trust on friendship alone, base it on mutual reciprocation of loyalty.

Protect yourself and the core of the business.

We've discuss the rings of protection. Now let's discuss your protection while pursuing your business journey. Your business is a vital part of your life. You work very hard building it and you deserve to keep it. But most of all, you need to protect the most critical asset of your business, the catalyst of your business—you. Most Small Business Owners/Entrepreneurs think that the only protection needed is for the business. False, you need to place all kinds of measures of protection for yourself.

You have to protect yourself from many obstacles, adversities and struggles that are mostly identified by the following but not exclusively:

- People that approach you for friendship and business partnering once they see success in the making.
- People that negotiate services, resources and goods for false persuasion of support only to take what you have achieved in business. These individuals are very aggressive in their pursuit, so be extremely careful of these types of people.
- Get rich quick fast deals.
- Immediate fast pace partnering arrangements by people you do not know.
- People that continuously feed off of your knowledge and never provide any of their knowledge.
- Once you reach a public level of approved success, don't let detractors expose you to the media or public eye without written consent of mutual benefits of all parties.
- People that try very hard to befriend you when you have noticed that they only want your business experience, business secrets of success, business ideas or that they only are looking out for themselves.
- People that are loud talkers in the crowd. These individuals most of the time want to be seen in the public eye and they are normally the ones that will go after your ideas.

When protecting yourself in business, always make sure you protect the core ideas of your business. Remember that if you do not maintain the security of your ideas, then someone else will benefit from them.

Most Small Business Owners/Entrepreneurs have superior abilities of selection when it comes to choosing the right people to involve in his or her business, but make certain not to repeat the mistakes of others. Plan, assess and evaluate every aspect of your business interactions. My advice to all of the Small Business Owners/Entrepreneurs is to follow your first thought about people and don't second-guess yourself. If you second-guess yourself, most likely you will open the opportunity for problems into your entrepreneurial journey.

Legal expectations

As Small Business Owners/Entrepreneurs, we tend to not maintain our legal representation to the highest standards because we think since we are small that there is no need for many things to be legally bounded. From experience, always seek legal support for every single business dealing. Never assume anything is too small for legal review or approval. Hold yourself accountable to the highest standards of legal expectations. I hear all around the Nation small business owners/entrepreneurs say, "I can't afford it." or "My business is too small." or "I can do it myself." Ask yourself this, "Can I afford the lawsuit or could I have avoided this legal battle if I had my Attorney look at this agreement?" Hire an Attorney the first day of your business creation and only use that legal representative when needed.

Make certain you maintain all documents, records, files and supporting documentation for everything. Make certain you maintain great employee records. Never represent yourself on a legal matter. Use an Attorney! To help you avoid the pain, disappointments and suffering of legal battles, <u>here are some</u> <u>suggestions to maintain in your day-to-day functions of your</u> <u>business as follows:</u>

- Don't assume that agreements are okay, have an Attorney review and approve all agreements.
- Legally document every transaction, transition and business matter.
- Before you release any information from your business to another, make certain you develop a legal binding agreement between all parties.
- Never sign a legal document without having an Attorney review it first.
- Always have a witness validate, sometimes a Notary, to verify your business signings between anybody you are doing business with no matter who they are, even if they are family or friends.
- When handling cash, credit, credit cards, business loans or lines of credit with one or more professionals in or out of your organization, <u>absolutely, at all times, have an Attorney</u> <u>make certain that you and your business are protected.</u>
- Get to know an Attorney from different perspectives of your business so that if you ever should need help, they will be readily available. ***Tip:*** *<u>Try to get them on your Board of</u>* *<u>Directors or Advisory Board</u>*!

From the start of your business and throughout the entire process of your business, make certain you handle all business interactions with employees with the support of an Attorney and rules, regulations and laws within Human Resources Guidelines.

Always conduct employee business with complete transparency. Make certain you always have one or more individuals (Human Resources or Legal) in the meeting to discuss employee business with an employee.

PART VII

INNOVATIVE RESOURCES!

Chapter 11

The Strategic Resources

Advisory Board

No business is too small to benefit from having an Advisory Board; it is such a powerful management tool that no small business should be without one. Most Small Business Owners/Entrepreneurs either think that an Advisory Board is too expensive to create, out of their reach or merely don't understand what it is and lack the complete understanding of its importance. I am going to explain to you what, why, when and how you should create an Advisory Board. I am going to provide you with the importance of an Advisory Board relating to the success or failure of your business and the great business advantages.

What is an Advisory Board?

Most definitions of an Advisory Board are truly the same, but what lacks is the board's importance, its creation and its positioning in business. Strategic Teaming is really the creator of an Advisory Board.

If you develop your business structure correctly, you will find out that an Advisory Board will provide you unlimited resources such as:

- Expert advice
- Broader network
- Path for business growth
- Structure for your direction to success
- Competitive Advantage
- Competitive Intelligence
- Better procurement penetration
- Better Marketing
- Better Business Development

Having an effective advisory board is critical to organizational success. An advisory board plays an instrumental role in marketing, business development, public relations and provides a fresh perspective on program issues. An advisory board works directly with the CEOs, Business Owners, Entrepreneurs and Directors to brainstorm, discuss, debate and decide major organizational decisions.

Wikipedia definition:

An **advisory board** is a body that advises the management of a corporation, organization, or foundation. Unlike the Board of Directors, the advisory board does not have authority to vote on corporate matters, nor a legal fiduciary responsibility. Many new or small businesses choose to have advisory boards in order to benefit from the knowledge of others, without the expense or formality of the Board of Directors.

Entrepreneur definition:

An advisory board is made up of volunteers who offer their input, ideas and expert advice to an organization's elected board of directors and shareholders.

BusinessDictionary.com definition:

Individuals appointed to offer expert advice to the elected board of directors. They are neither bound by the legal duties imposed on the elected board members, nor are the elected board bound by their recommendations.

Advisory Board Member Roles

A key to building a secure organization is having an independent advisory board of industry leaders, expert business professionals, seasoned and experienced professionals and other interested people that align with your business. Advisory board members are volunteers and should reflect diversified representation from various cultures, socioeconomic groups and urban and rural environments.

Some advisory board members take responsibility for specific, mission-oriented tasks while others only attend meetings and provide input and feedback. All members are expected to carry out a specific function independently. An advisory member's focus should be helping the CEOs, Board of Directors, Business Owners and Entrepreneurs with certain responsibilities such as business development, branding, marketing and other areas of the business. Certain advisory board members should be your eyes and ears when it comes to preliminary penetration of your targeted market segment. Both boards should work in a team effort with the organization's best interests in mind.

Advisory board members usually attend board meetings each year in-person, video or conference call to share information, discuss ideas and make decisions. Once a structure is in place, the board can distribute its governing functions and responsibilities equally among its members to maximize its effectiveness. The advisory board members can provide you with important intelligence to provide you with more effective and innovative means to reach your success for the business. You should use them to create your pipelines, network growth and strategic business awareness. They also allow you to generate a great knowledge base resource tool for the market.

Advisory Board Members Duties and Responsibilities

- Advisory board members join an organization for a limited amount of time and pledge their personal, professional and financial resources to help assist in your business mission. Advisory board member duties and responsibilities are assigned at the discretion of the CEO, Business Owner, President or Board of Directors. Some responsibilities typically assigned to an advisory board member include:
  o Attend meetings
  o Branding
  o Contribute input and feedback
  o Create programs and policies
  o Develop business strategies
  o Develop subcommittees
  o Marketing

o Organizational development

o Planning, fund-raising and community relations

o Promotional Ideas and public awareness

o Strategic planning and decision making

Advisory Board Member Orientation and Training:

Advisory board members need to understand an organization to serve it effectively. Giving tasks to new members will allow them to develop a sense of belonging and help them become more involved. Every board member will need ongoing training to remain current on organizational issues. This can be accomplished at scheduled board meetings, webinars and other organizational sponsored events.

Board members should receive public recognition for the important volunteer work that they do for the organization. Holding an annual recognition benefit or dinner is an easy and fun way to recognize board members and volunteers for the hard work and support they provide you throughout the year. You could also be creative and provide monetary bonuses, paid vacation trips and other incentives of appreciation. Ensure that board members understand their individual roles and have the necessary resources to carry out their duties. You should identify the skills needed for your organization and recruit and train board members based on those needs.

HOW TO FORM A STRATEGIC ADVISORY BOARD

To develop the framework and to form a strategic advisory board, you have to define the purpose and function of the board. You have to decide what kind of support you need in alignment with your business both internally and externally.

<u>The purpose of the Advisory Board should be composed of several important factors as follows:</u>

- Make certain that your advisory board serves the purpose of providing information, resources and support that you are not able to obtain on your own; something that is out of your reach.
- Make certain that every one of your advisory board members is reliable, trustworthy and dedicated to supporting your organization.
- Make certain that your advisory board members are strategically knowledgeable in the areas that you need their expertise for business support.
- Make certain they understand the perimeters of support that outline your business needs.
- Make certain you execute agreements between yourself, your company and all advisory board members.
- To generate additional knowledge and credibility for your business, utilize resources to obtain and expedite targeted opportunities needed for your business success.

Your framework for your strategic advisory board should be defined as to what you need to get you to the levels of success for your business now and in the future. You need to design your advisory board for legal protection and legal support resources so that you can get ahead of the legal issues that may arise in your everyday business affairs. The forming of your strategic advisory board should be designed to provide you additional layers of industry expertise and business experience that has proven successes. Don't place a person on your advisory board because they seem successful, make certain they have "walked the walk" and not just "talked the talk;" in other words, make absolutely sure they have achieved what you need.

Make sure that your strategic advisory board is composed of measures of alignment with an interchange of information that has proven past and future resources of knowledge to get your business through issues it may encounter and resources that bring solutions to any upcoming, unforeseen problems.

Next, start your advisory board off small, but strategic in providing extended solutions for your business alignment for growth and knowledge. It is easy to add board members, but don't add them for the sake of saying you have an advisory board. Have an advisory board that serves with a purpose. It's not legally difficult to remove an advisory board member from your board, but it's sensitive and delicate since these are likely individuals you have held with high regard and you most likely asked them for support and to be on your board. You don't want to create a bad exiting of your members. This can cause problems for your business immediately or in the near future.

The ultimate question for many of you will be how many advisory board members should I start out with on my board? Should they be located nearby? Should they be friends, relatives or what level of mutual business relationship? A great start is at least one. You will hear that 4 or 5 advisory board members are too many until you grow. Don't believe this because you will need as many advisory members as possible to ensure your expanded business knowledge and growth. Remember that Advisory Board Members bring added knowledge, resources and expertise to your business. Okay, now ask yourself this, what kind of added business strength of knowledge do I need? What kind of doors do I need opened? What relationships do I need? Well, these are a part of your answers as to why you need an advisory board and the value they can bring to your business.

Remember, you can add advisory board members whenever you choose to do so for your business.

Your framework should be defined by a charter or covenant detailing what you want the board to do, how the board will work and what is expected from the board. Again, as mentioned, make certain your attorney is involved in the process to cover any legal matters or concerns of the board development. You can always change, delete or add functions to the board, but make certain you keep everyone informed.

You should define structure in your framework through the following:

- How frequently will the board meet, personally or via conference call?
- Any compensation for the board members, but it doesn't have to be monetary; it could be gift cards, dinners, etc.
- Board requirements
- Guidelines, restrictions and limitations
- Other areas as needed to define your particular business advisory board framework

A word of advice: Create an Advisory Board for your business. Do not take shortcuts and start the process day 1 of your business. Actually, you should already have in mind who you want to place on your board. Create a list of requirements for your advisory board members to meet so that you know you are getting the minimum requisite needed in your layer vetting process.

BENEFICAL REASONS TO START AN ADVISORY BOARD

From experience, one of the best assets to create for your business is "Teaming" and then an "Advisory Board." For both of my companies, as the core of my strategic structure of Teaming, I immediately developed an Advisory Board. Ironically in prior, high-level contracted positions that I held, I developed everything from a "Teaming" perspective combined with a form of an "Advisory Board" to the completion of the project and mission to success. Have you ever thought about setting up an Advisory Board? It can be one of the best moves you make for your business. And it is easier than you think—costing little or nothing.

Make this your initial mission as part of your creation and setup of your business.

Here are some of greatest reasons to set a Strategic Advisory Board:

Expertise, experience and resources you can't buy or place a price on:

Advisory Board members can bring skill sets that are totally out of reach for many small businesses that can cost more than most small businesses can afford.

Let's use an example of an Advisory Board for a small technology business. The Advisory Board Members are:

- Attorney or Law Firm
- Bank Executive
- Current or retired CEO, COO, CIO, CKO, CTO or other experienced and knowledgeable professional needed for your business.
- Finance manager with Fortune 100 or 500 experience
- Former Government Official
- Former Political Official
- University professor

Can you imagine what it would cost you to hire these professionals of such high skill levels, experience and knowledge? Most small businesses would not be able to afford these resources even after they won contracts. The question is why should you even attempt to pay for such services? Be smart! A carefully chosen Advisory Board can give you access to such people for a tiny fraction of that cost—or no cost. Most of the time, the only expense comes from convening meetings, air travel, food, hotels, rental cars and other supporting resources. If you think innovatively about your structure by Teaming, you can get all of the needed supporting resources paid for by the advisory board members. Remember, you do not have to physically have a meeting in person to get advice from your members; you could instead pick up the phone or email the members.

Business connections when you need them:

You should select your Advisory Board Members with diverse backgrounds and a strategic alignment for your business and their connections will become one of your most valuable assets for reaching your business goals. When you pick the right Advisory Board Members, they will be very interested in your business success and they will make every effort to introduce you to important people they feel will help your business grow.

Advisory Board Members can introduce you to people that can be the door openers to business that may have previously been closed. The doors that you may not have ever been able to open or doors that you never knew even existed that could help your business.

You should obtain Advisory Board Members that have relationship connections that can produce the following resources for your business:

* Potential Investors
* Professionals that can get you to the targeted procurements needed for your business
* Future clients
* Bank representatives
* Many more resources that align with your business to help it grow

The Resources and Benefits of a Board of Directors without the hassles

Some Small Business Owners/Entrepreneurs think an Advisory Board is the same as a Board of Directors. Yet, some really do not know what a Board of Directors really provide for businesses. You should understand that an Advisory Board has many more outstanding benefits than a Board of Directors and a lot more flexibility for your business. They can make your mission come to life much easier. As described in the definitions earlier in this chapter, an Advisory Board is exactly what the name suggests: they simply are present to advise or provide advice for your business. This means you inherent the benefits of your advisory board members, without all the formalities, intrusiveness and great expense of a Board of Directors. Board of Directors are great for reasons of making critical decisions of your business to reach its growth, but they are defined with far greater formal authority and power within your business.

- Advisory Board members have no formal authority or power within your business, unlike Board of Directors.
- An Advisory Board doesn't have the same legal responsibilities (fiduciary) as a Board of Directors. That means you won't need to pay the high costs/fees and provide Board of Directors Insurance coverage to protect them from liability exposure that will impact your business.
- You will not have to observe legal formalities for meetings, such as voting, etc. With a Board of Directors, you will have to provide mandatory meetings, voting for business decisions, legal procedures for business meetings and most of the time you will have to provide paid positions or equity of your business or a combination thereof.
- You do not have to share or reveal your business' financial details to an Advisory Board, but sometimes you may need to. For example, you should provide financial info if you have a financial advisory board member that is trying to help you with funding for your business, financial support for your contracts or working out cost/profit for a potential contract opportunity. With a Board of Directors, you are

normally required or committed to revealing your financials to them.

Easy, Simple, Strategic and inexpensive to set up and operate

Advisory Boards are relatively easy to set up and operate. You can construct as informal or formal an advisory board as needed. You have total flexibility. You can streamline and align your advisory board for your business as simple as having a couple of breakfast, lunch or dinner meetings. You can be strategically structured to have regular meetings once a month, every other month, once a quarter, or twice a year with defined agendas to accomplish your mission for your business. You can get a tremendous amount of help from Advisory Board Members in an extremely inexpensive manner. You want to use your Advisory Board in a very useful manner because this is a vital resource that can help your business excel. Remember the level of formality and structure is totally up to you for your business. Maximize your benefits to maximize your clarity of business success.

How much does it cost to have an Advisory Board? What are the expenses? What is the operational cost for maintaining an advisory board? Well, most Advisory Boards serve for free and will not accept money for services. They just want to donate time and support some type of business that will help others or merely a business that will provide a legacy for them. You should always reimburse your Advisory Board Members for out-of-pocket expenses, travel, mileage and other related business expenses. Pay for lunch or breakfast meetings you may have with them, at a minimum. Small Business Owners/Entrepreneurs typically call on friends and colleagues who are willing to help out and some are excited to be asked.

But be very careful asking friends and colleagues to be an Advisory Board Member because it may not cost you anything initially to get them, but it may cost you a lifetime of misery if you do not make certain that they acknowledge the following:

- Understand your business and be willing to really support your business.
- Be grounded in trust and loyalty to you and your business.
- Have your best interest at heart for you and your business.
- They are business-oriented in a mindset to truly understand business.
- Aligned and educated about your business to be able to provide you with the correct advisement or advice.
- Have a full understanding of your business' day-to-day operations.

Fast Track Business Growth

An Advisory Board is a great way to get your business to success at a much faster pace.

You can accelerate your business growth by means of having an Advisory Board by development of "Teaming" such as:

- Validated business relationships between potential client representatives and yourself when you do not even know who the client representatives are in that particular client organizational structure

- Teaming by Credibility™ by the strength of credibility to client acceptance
- Marketing and Branding penetration without even pursuit to market
- Business Development penetration to the marketplace

Only businesses that are serious about growth or truly understanding of the importance of an Advisory Board take the time and effort to organize an Advisory Board. When you develop your advisory board, make certain all members of your board are strategic in their experience and mindset. Individuals whose judgment you respect fully and who have strategic thinking abilities are who you should have on your Advisory Board. Do not accept anything less than excellence and total strategic business alignment. ***Business-to-Teaming-to-Advisory Board-to-Success!***

Your listening audience

Advisory Board Members can serve as your audience before the show! You want to perform well in the world of business. So why not create an internal audience that can make certain you are at your highest performance levels to reach your highest levels of success? This just makes a lot of business sense. Your Advisory Board can create new ideas and solve difficult problems. What you want to create is an Advisory Board that can eliminate problems before they exist!

Some of the major qualities that an Advisory Board member should possess are that they are eagerly willing to keep your best interest as a priority and they are trusted, informed listeners and supporters. A lot of times as a Small Business Owner/Entrepreneur, you need someone to talk who will only listen. They may be able to direct or lead you to creative and innovative solutions that are very simple that you may have simply overlooked while being in the trenches of business. You can receive lessons learned from your advisory board members to avoid going through certain adversities, struggles or obstacles you may come upon.

Mentoring and Coaching

Your Advisory Board Members should be a source of mentoring and coaching for your business. When I initially thought about strategically seeking mentors, I thought of the many resources I could achieve from them and I kept coming back to the same resources designed and provided by Advisory Board. That's when I realized that my design of an "Advisory Board by Teaming (ABT)" was a multiple resource of many solutions. **Example:** *I went to speak with one of my largest Subcontractors' (Fortune 100 Company) CEO to ask for mentorship. He listened to what I had to say on my request of mentorship. He then began to explain to me that I had more mentorship that he could ever provide. What he stated was that not only did I have him and his 29,000 employee support staff behind me, but I had every resource of support with hundreds of other subcontractors of like and similar type companies.*

I had created a "Mentorship of Many by Teaming (MMT)" that produced all types of mentoring capabilities.

Here are some of the mentoring capabilities that derived from my "Strategic Core of Teaming (SCT)" as follows:

- Personal Professional Development (PPP)

- Strategic Financial Support (SFS)
- Strategic Innovative Methods (SIMS)
- Innovative Strategic Processes (ISP)

You should think of your Advisory Board Members as mentors in various specialty areas. Basically, your mentors coach you to become stronger and better leaders. They motivate and inspire you to greater leadership levels through their own positive ways. They help you get through the tough times of business while supporting and encouraging you to succeed. Small Business Owners/ Entrepreneurs often have few ways to get support, direction and guidance and this is why you should develop a "Teaming Structure" to achieve advisory boards, mentors, resources, coaching, etc.

Now that you see all of the benefits of an Advisory Board, are you going to create one? Create your Advisory Board at the initial start of your business. Don't wait!

Economics

It is extremely important as a Small Business Owner/Entrepreneur to fully understand your targeted market, market segmentation, industry and economic conditions. You need to be very knowledgeable of business economics that surround your business environment. The major, current economic conditions related to your business determine your business' growth and success.

To stay abreast of your business environment, you need to stay current with the economic indicators that impact your business for growth and provides you the current information to adjust your business operations to adjust with the strategic alignment of reaching success.

You need to fully understand where to obtain important data for your business that can define the guidelines on how and what methods you need to meet certain economic conditions.

<u>Here are a few important places to find economic data and trending to be strategic in your business growth:</u>

- United States Department of Commerce—Economics and Statistics Administration (ESA): This is where you can find Principal Federal Economic Indicators.
- www.EconomicIndicators.gov is where you can find economic indicators.
- U.S. Census Bureau and the Bureau of Economic Analysis (BEA)

<u>The website www.businessusa.gov is where you can find basic information as follows:</u>

- o Starting a Business
- o Growing your Business
- o Access to Financing
- o Exporting
- o Expanding Exporting
- o Finding Opportunities
- o Resources for Veterans
- o Disaster Assistance
- o Health Care Changes
- o Taxes and Credits

There are many more places to find important economic data for your business. Perform your due diligence and research your business and industry efficiently.

Do you know what really drives the U.S. economy? It is not military campaigns, not large companies, not politics. These things do impact the economic in a tremendous way. However, small business firms with fewer than 500 employees drive the U.S. economy by providing jobs for over half of the nation's private workforce.

Politics

Small Business Politics & Public Policy

As Small Business Owners/Entrepreneurs, we know we have to be strategic, innovative and consistently sharp in our pursuit to business success. But we should also know that we have to constantly execute our due diligence to maintain current on our always changing political issues in this country. We have to lead by example and take charge of our own future when it comes to strategic business planning and day-to-day operations in our businesses. You will hear people say, "But now, more than ever before in our lives, the business world is enthralled in politics and as a Small Business Owner/Entrepreneur, we have to get involved much more." Well, this is true and you should always stay current in politics, but once you make that decision to be a Small Business Owner/Entrepreneur, you must get heavily involved in public policy. Your attitude of running your business should be the same as placing priority on being knowledgeable on public policy.

Whether you know it or not, small businesses provide more than 50% of the nation's workforce and stands to be a "Political Force" not to be reckoned with in the United States. But also, small businesses have a devastating failure rate of over 85% in their second year of business. The third year gets even worse. But in the last few years, small business ratios of failure have decreased greatly and success rates have increased slightly. Small Businesses are gaining momentum as a class in the United States, as well as other parts of the world, to be the innovator of business. Politicians are becoming highly aware of our critical segment as a forward frontier toward the future.

We all must become more involved in the political process. If we don't, there will be laws passed that is not of our best interest that will impact our businesses for the worse. We have rights that constitute great powers of persuasion to get laws passed, but if we decide not to get involved, then we will have no right to complain when a law is passed that negatively affects our businesses. What happens when we come together is that the government will no longer have the overruling power to pass laws without regard for how it affects us. Get involved in public policy right now to position for the future!

The current political party in charge today is doing a great job for small businesses even based on the hard economic times. Regardless of what you hear or what your political views are today or tomorrow, you have to work with the current political administration and whoever it may be in the future.

You can take the time, which will be a losing period of time in your business, arguing what may not be in your best personal or political interest, but place all personal opinions aside to support our President Barack Obama and his Staff to drive better small business resources to support our country in unity. *Don't get caught up in fighting a war of politically biased views, but come together as one and fight as a multi-dimensional, diverse strength of the United States.* The fight to move our businesses to the foremost position of success is our greatest pursuit, but implement it in a manner of smart, innovative thinking and execution to project a better tomorrow and future for all businesses.

Marketing and Social Media

It is extremely important in our highly advanced technological business environment today and in the future, to have a thoughtful and thorough small business Strategic Marketing Plan in conjunction with an innovative Social Media Strategy. You have to really research and fully understand your industry marketplace and retain great knowledge capture to creatively be able to develop a great path of vision and exposure to your potential client/customer audience.

To develop an effective Small Business Marketing Social Media Strategy, you have to creatively design an innovative means of strategic planning to fit your business niche to the interest of your audience.

Here are some of the major degrees to development of a "Marketing Social Media Strategy":

Major Degree #1: Identify your audience and your strategic objectives:

- Define your targeted audience and what may connect you to them in a way of exposing your products/services to their paths of need. You have to define their needs and place your products/services in niche manner that would fit their need with less transition of collaboration. A smooth injection of external services into an internal system creates a great blended solution.
- Develop a Social Media Strategy that places you at the forefront of your targeted audience's sights as follows:
  - Strategic Branding by "Teaming" to gain the maximum name recognition. Think about it: You can't buy the credibility you can gain by having someone that is well-connected and respected in the industry to validate you in the industry to your client base. "OBT Strategic Teaming™"
  - Tactic of selling your product/service directly only by credibility of indirect strategies of credibility. "OBT Strategic Teaming™"
  - Incentives to enhance special unique offers, coupons, free pre-assessments, presentations and innovative QR Codes to drive incentives.
  - Website magnetism—Creation of unique attraction to bring your targeted clients/customers to your website to provide solutions for their needs.

○ Ratio of goal accomplishments to gain targeted client/ customer traffic to your products/services via your website.

Major Degree #2: <u>Define and identify a method to market to your targeted audience using the correct Platforms:</u>

- Your defining method will be revealed once you define your targeted audience and business group separation such as:
  ○ Information Technology business with $1 Billion in revenue
  ○ Risk Management business with minimum of 15,000 employees with revenue of $10 Billion
- Once you determine the targeted audience, key shareholders or stakeholders, environment and other pertinent data, then you will proceed to define where your targeted audience actively shares their usage of products/services and how they interact and communicate on particular platforms such as follows:
  ○ BlogSpot
  ○ Facebook
  ○ Google
  ○ LinkedIn
  ○ Twitter
  ○ Wikipedia
  ○ You Tube

Major Degree #3: <u>Becoming visual and having great presence</u> <u>on the Social Media Platform:</u>

- Determining your business value to provide a great proposition for your targeted audience. Example: Make certain your website is constructed correctly to provide whatever results you are aiming for such as driving traffic to your site or capturing retainable information to provide a network listing.
- Whatever platform you decide to use, make certain it is aligned with the availability of allowance to market what you need accomplished. Make certain you know the limitations of that particular platform.

Major Degree #4: <u>Making certain that information maintains a</u> <u>critical value and creates a vital niche and need:</u>

- In order for your content to stay at a maximum, you have to make certain it generates a vital need, niche or desire for the mass targeted audience.
- To become valuable to the platform, you have to post useful information, but most importantly, you are contributing to the platform to gain credibility. Easiest way to accomplish this is by "Teaming" to build a strong relationship and credibility. But you must establish the relationship first, build upon it and maintain it. Remember, regular distribution of data on the platform makes you highly searchable to the platform mass.

- Most of all, to maintain the competitive advantage, you have to tell the audience to reach you on the credible platform by means of what you can provide them, detail of what you are providing and make certain it is built with credibility.

- Like all aspects of your business, always set a timeframe to measure and check your results. Social Media takes a lot of time and patience, but the payoff for your business is far greater than even traditional marketing.

Travel

This is a critical area usage for your business that can be a great competitive advantage or it can be an incredible abyss to toss all of your hard earned money down for your business and personally. As a Small Business Owner/Entrepreneur, you have to be extremely precise in your spending, remain budget conscious, but highly flexible on directing your money to highly vital travel events, meetings, conferences, seminars, teaming building and other reasonable related spending.

Here are several important tips and considerations to maximize your small business travel needs:

- When traveling and delayed in airports, you should maximize your time by utilizing the VIP Clubs such as the Admiral Club, the Emerald Club, etc. The reason you benefit from these services is that you can have secure meetings, conference calls, computer and printing services and produce work even in a stalled environment. This will be a great added value if you and/or your employees travel a lot and spend a lot of time in airports. Normally, you get a great price point if you are associated with various airline frequent flyer programs, veteran programs, business clubs or groups, etc.

* When traveling on airplanes, it may be very valuable for you and your employees to work and have Wi-Fi availability, but again, if you are a frequent traveler then you will maximize the value of spending on Wi-Fi service versus value-add. Remember to buy services in longer term periods to maximize savings.

* Make certain you are traveling on your trips with a clear purpose and that the conferences are precisely what your business needs. There are so many conferences, seminars, symposiums that do not meet the standards of what they state you will receive from them. Do extensive research to define the right business event for your business.

* Importantly, spend the money to cultivate precise and strategic teaming relationships. This is very important because it will produce resources for every aspect of your business.

Chapter 12

The Journey Begins

Now that you have thought long and hard about becoming an Entrepreneur and Small Business Owner, you have to commit to the journey of a lifetime. Never look at your entrepreneurial journey as something that you will try out or get your feet wet. Take your entrepreneurial journey very seriously because there are very critical responsibilities, vital time consumption, adversities, obstacles, roadblocks, struggles and possible hardships that may become evident throughout your business pursuit.

You have to understand that the ultimate outcome is "Success" and the questions I pose to you from the beginning are as follows:

- Do you really want to take this entrepreneurial journey?
- Are you willing take the total responsibility of whatever comes your way in business?
- Are you a patient person? If not, then you need to re-evaluate your patience level because business is a test of your patience.
- Will you invest in your business? If not, how do you expect anyone else to want to invest in your business?

Be generous if you are going to accomplish greatness. But don't be naive in simply believing in hearsay about business, instead do your due diligence and gain invaluable knowledge. If you are willing to put unlimited efforts to build your business with substantial limitations, then you should pursue your business journey.

Words of Wisdom:

"Your dream will remain a mere image of what it could be, unless you strive to achieve it no matter what struggles, obstacles or adversity come your way."

Operation Breakthrough
Strategies Corporation!

(An Entrepreneurial and Small Business Owner's Solutions Consulting Firm)

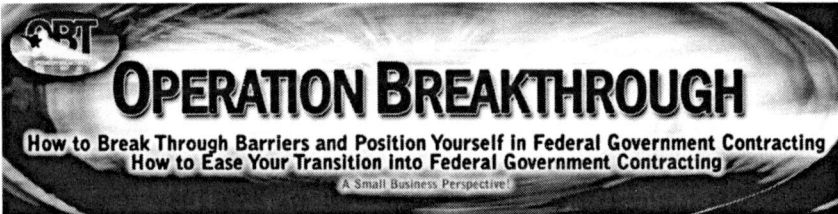

OPERATION BREAKTHROUGH

How to Break Through Barriers and Position Yourself in Federal Government Contracting
How to Ease Your Transition into Federal Government Contracting
A Small Business Perspective!

OPERATION TEAMING: BARRIER BREAKING STRATEGICALLY

Business Transformation in all Areas of Life!

When you are having an discussion about reaching your goals of success for your business, how to develop your business, which direction do I pursue, how do I gain the developmental tools needed for my business, what approach should I use, what are my challenges, how do I team with others and who should I team with and how do I conduct business overall to my road of success.

"Operation Breakthrough Strategies" provides a complete innovative business solution to help any Small Business Owner and Entrepreneur in their pursuit to success no matter what industry or type of business service offerings or products. We provide a multi-functional and multi-solutions business approach for all business requirements. Let us help you! We will provide not only small business solutions to success, but we will provide you a great deal of savings in the process.

"Operation Breakthrough Strategies" was developed by CEO/ President: Nate Couser, CPT., AWSIM. He developed a platform of "TEAMING" and a unique "BUSINESS PROCESS" like no other organization or company in the country. While cultivating his teaming relationships throughout his career and at the creation and continuance of his company, he developed the nucleus of his business model. His business model known as "Teaming" is a business platform that offers Small Business Solutions, Teaming, Business Basics, Business Advance techniques, Strategic Networking, Innovative Business Matchmaking, and lots of resources for every small business industry type. This business platform and program process should be the model to adopt in the alignment of your business now and in the future.

We help all small, medium and large business types such as:

"Start-ups" "Emerging Small Businesses"
"Women-Owned Small Businesses"
"Service-Disabled Veteran-Owned Small Businesses"
"Veteran-Owned Small Businesses"
"HUB Zone Businesses"
"8A Businesses"
"Minority-Owned Businesses"
"Medium & Large Businesses"

We have clients that start with an idea (1-person) to several individuals; all size business types from 10 to 20,000 employees and provide total business developmental support throughout their business journey whether being in business from 1 to 20 plus years. We have helped clients start building out their business from an idea, developing that idea into a business plan-model and straight to implementation-operation and execution.

THE PROCESS:

* *We provide an initial consultation and then a pre-assessment to determine if we can provide help for your business.*

* *Then we provide extensive "Assessments and Evaluations" to validate that your business has a "Niche versus Need" for your particular industry.*

* *Then we proceed with a 1-3 year detailed customized program for a complete overall developmental business implementation with total support throughout to help each business achieve their success.*

We provide guidance in all areas of business to help the many Entrepreneurs and Small Business Owners reach their goals to accomplish great success. We have already helped businesses develop an entire practice, total business foundation-structure-operations to complete success of winning contracts in the millions and billions. We are a proven business concept of successful solutions.

Our Mottos:

"Changing the Wave of the Future by Innovativeness"

"Breaking through Barriers in Public & Private Sector Contracting"

"Teaming by Credibility"

"A Small, Medium & Large Business Perspective to Success"

"The How to Approach to Business Success in any industry for Products, Services and Solutions"

Questions to measure your Entrepreneurial Journey Expectations!

Questions for Pre/Post entrepreneurs and small business owners:

- What is Success?
- How do you measure Success?
- What is your level of success?
- How do you achieve success for your business?
- What is an Entrepreneur? What are your responsibilities?
- What protection do you have in place as an "Entrepreneur/ Small Business Owner?"
- What is a Business Plan? How often do you use it? Update it?
- What is Creditability?
- Do you have a Niche versus Need Business opportunity and does it fit your marketplace?
- Does anyone know what "Layering" your company means?
- What is a "Structure" for your business?
- Are you ready to actually do business? Are you equipped with the proper tools?
- How will you handle adversity, obstacles, barriers, setbacks, hurdles and downfalls?
- How much do you budget for Marketing, Social Media, Business Development and Resource Building?
- Do you know your Marketplace Sector?

○ How do you get through the struggles and failures to achieve success?

○ Are you willing to fail or be consistent in your pursuit of success?

○ How often should you measure your business success and at what level do you assess yourself?

○ Who should you trust in your pursuit of business?

○ What conferences, seminars, symposiums and events should you attend for your business?

○ What key accomplishments actually make your business contract-ready?

○ Should you seek Legal Assistance for your business and if so, when should you inquire about these services?

○ What does doing your homework mean prior to doing business? While doing business? And after you receive the level of success you are striving for in your business pursuit?

○ Does diversity place a major role in your business pursuit?

○ Does discrimination play a factor in doing business and if so, how do you break that barrier?

○ Does the economy play a role in your business for success and/or failure?

○ Do politics play a role in your business pursuit?

○ What does your business structure look like in the frame of things?

○ As an Entrepreneur, do you provide respect to gain respect or do you demand respect?

○ What is the culture of your business?

○ What is the difference between an "Entrepreneur" and "Small Business Owner?"

Appendix C

About the Author

NATHANIEL COUSER (NATE), Veteran Army Captain, Joint Warfighter

"Destined to win by God! To have Favor and Full of Faith!

Nathaniel Couser is the CEO/President and founder of **NASTEP Consulting Corporation**, a global, multi-functional, Veteran-Owned Small Business National Defense Contractor and **Operation Breakthrough Strategies Corporation,** a national, multi-functional, business consulting solutions service firm of multi-solutions and structure for business building. This firm is diversified, fast-paced, innovative, solutions-oriented and established to provide clients with accurate, on-target and precise project development through creation of a "One Source-One Solution" focus. His goal is to ensure that the company utilizes cutting-edge technology in every contract secured by incorporating a wide range of capabilities with the assistance in collaborating with our highly capable teaming partners.

Nate formed a multi-functional, high-level competitive intelligence team to ensure that all capabilities under our contracts and for our clients could easily be achieved and successfully delivered with an upward mobility of enhanced organizational development to accomplish any future task at a high level of execution.

After more than 29 years in the Public, Military and Private Business Sector, Nate has created an industry "niche to need" and has very strong, proven processes on what it takes to get to high levels of success regardless of business size or industry. Understanding the entrepreneurial journey and the fact that "failure is never an option," Nate has created an extensive path along the way—heading off obstacles, going strategically through barriers and roadblocks, breaking through walls, opening doors he thought were closed and various other struggles to try and eliminate most of the entrepreneur's targeted successes.

From serving in the U.S. Army and Reserves, National Guard, United States Atlantic Command and United States Joint Forces Command, being a prior Joint Warfighter and supporting the Joint Warfighter, Military and Government Agencies, Private Sector and working in many different industries, he understands and has accomplished more than 29 plus years of engineering, telecommunications, information technology, information security, human capital solutions, program and project management, various phases of consulting management, financial management, vendor management office solutions, strategy and operations, staffing and research and development experience.

In his community and nationally, Nate has been recognized as a business leader, small business solutions expert, success story, strategist and has received global recognitions from many entities. Nate has accumulated over 1000 Teaming Partner relationships to maximize support nationally and abroad in a myriad of industries.

Appendix D

Abbreviations

The Glossary is protected by Nate Couser of Operation Breakthrough Strategies Corporation. All rights reserved. All abbreviations listed in appendix contains copyright© laws governed by Nate Couser of Operation Breakthrough Strategies Corporation.

Abbreviations:

(1) 3 Point Check System (OBT3PCS© or 3PCS©)

(2) Additive Intelligence Tool© (AIT)

(3) Advanced Innovative Intelligence© **(AII)**

(4) Advisory Board by Teaming (ABT)

(5) After Action Plan (AAP)

(6) Art of OBT Teaming© (AOBTT)

(7) Business & Personal Protection System© (BPPS)

(8) Business Building Model Concept (BBMC)

(9) Business Development by Credibility (BDC)

(10) Checking System of Validation© (CSV)

(11) Circle of Affiliation (COA)

(12) Circle of Knowledge (COK)

(13) Collaborated Strategic Partnership (CSP)

(14) Competitive Forward Intelligence© **(CFI)**

(15) Conference Competitive Intelligence (CCI)

(16) Conference Associated and Cost (CAC©) versus Knowledge Business Advancement© (KBA©)

(17) Connection of Communication© **(COC)**

(18) Credibility for Branding and Marketing© **(CBM)**

(19) Credibility for Marketplace Penetration© **(CMP)**

(20) **Credibility by Teaming™©** or Credibility by OBT Teaming™© **(CBT)**

(21) **Data Failure Chart© (DFC)**

(22) **Entrepreneurial Book Series™ (EBS™)**

(23) Extension Lateral Support (ELS) ©

(24) Failure of Alignment (FOA)

(25) Flags of Failure (FAF)

(26) Forecasting Method of Approach (FMA)

(27) Formula for Success© (FFS)

(28) Forward Collaborated Intelligence© **(FCI)**

(29) Generational Concept Connection© **(GCC)**

(30) **Generation Collaborative Breakthrough© (GCB)**

(31) Geographical Selective Positioning© **(GSP)**

(32) Innovative Strategic Processes (ISP)

(33) Innovative Team Approach (ITA)

(34) Intelligent Awareness Positioning© (IAP)

(35) Internal Personal Value (IPV)

(36) Inverted Upside Triangle Effect© or IUTE©

(37) Knowledge Support Structure (KSS)

(38) License to Hunt© **(LTH)**

(39) Logic of Thought (LOT)

(40) Longevity Committed Friends (LCF)

(41) Measure of Success (MOS)

(42) Mentorship by Teaming (MBT)

(43) Mentorship of Many by Teaming (MMT)

(44) Multi-Functional Process (OBTMFP™ or MFP©)

(45) Multi-Functional Strategy (OBTMFS© or MFS©)

(46) Multi-Functional Team (OBTMFT© or MFT™)

(47) Multi-Level Business Development (OBTMLBD© or MLBD©)

(48) Multi-Level Marketing (OBTMLM© or MLM©)

(49) Multi-Level Competitive Advancement (OBTMLCA© or MLCA©)

(50) Multi-Level Competitive Intelligence (OBTMLCI© or MLCI©)

(51) Multi-Level Opportunity Building (OBTMLOB© or MLOB©)

(52) Multi-Level Structure Building (OBTMLSB© or MLSB©)

(53) Networking Plan of Action (NPA)

(54) Niche for Necessity© **(NFN)**

(55) **Obstacles and Struggles (OAS)**

(56) **Operation Breakthrough: Entrepreneurial Paths to Success© (EPS)**

(57) Operation Breakthrough Strategies© **(OBS)**

(58) OBT Competitive Business Intelligence (OBTCBI© or CBI©)

(59) OBT Economic Strategies© or Economic Strategies (OBTES)

(60) OBT Perception to Progress™—(OBTPTP or PTP)

(61) OBT Strategic Teaming (OBTST or **OBT Teaming©** **or OBTS Teaming©)**

(62) **OBTS Structure Model© (OBTSSM)**

(63) **OBT Teaming for Credibility™ (OBTTFC)**

(64) Operational Structure Penetration (OSP) also known as "Operation Breakthrough"

(65) Permit to be in Attendance© **(PBA)**

(66) Personal Professional Development (PPP)

(67) Phases of Success (PHS)

(68) **Planning a Priority© (PAP)**

(69) Positioning of Success© **(POS)**

(70) Precise Penetration Positioning© **(3Ps or PPP)**

(71) Prepare Prior to Pursuit of Anything© (PPPA)

(72) Prior Planning Prevents Poor Performance (5Ps or PPPPP)

(73) Proper Planning Prevents Poor Pursuit or Performance©" (6Ps or PPPPPP)

(74) Receipt of Understanding (ROU)

(75) Rules of Measurement (ROM)

(76) Screening Support Awareness Program (SSAP)

(77) Sensitive Compartmented Information Facility (SKIFF or SCIF)

(78) Small Business Successors© (SBS)

(79) **Stimulated Innovative Growth© (SIG)**

(80) Strategic Advisory Board (OBTSAB© or SAB©)

(81) Strategic Alignment of Positioning© **(SAP)**

(82) Strategic Core of Teaming (SCT)

(83) Strategic Credibility Program (SCP)

(84) Strategic Educational Instruction© **(SEI)**

(85) Strategic Financial Support (SFS)

(86) Strategic Impact Relationships© **(SIR)**

(87) Strategic Informational Method (SIM)

(88) Strategic Innovative Methods (SIMS)

(89) Strategic Knowledge Positioning© (SKP)

(90) Strategic Marketing by Credibility (SMC)

(91)   Strategic Order of Success© (SOOS)

(92)   Strategic Slow Overlapping Observation (SSOO)

(93)   Strategic Teaming to Tactical Success© (STTS) or OBTS Teaming

(94)   **Strife and Strive (SAS)**

(95)   Structure to Strategic System to Success (SSSS)

(96)   Support by Collaboration (SBC)

(97)   Sustainment Model for Success© **(SMS)**

(98)   System of Structure© **(SOS)**

(99)   Teaming (OBT Strategic Teaming)

(100)   Teaming by Credibility© **(TBC)**

(101)   Think, Technical & Tactical© **(TTT)**

(102)   Three-Check System (TCS) ©

(103)   Three-Step System (TSS) ©

(104)   Upward Strategic Support (USS) ©

(105)   Want-to-be-Friends (WTBF) ©

Appendix E

Entrepreneur and Small Business Owner's Inspirational Quotes

Read one inspirational quote per business day Monday through Friday and one on Saturday because like most of us Entrepreneurs and Small Business Owners we normally work on a lot of Saturdays. The Inspirational Quotes is protected by Nate Couser of Operation Breakthrough Strategies Corporation. All rights reserved. All inspirational quotes listed in appendix contains copyright© laws governed by Nate Couser of Operation Breakthrough Strategies Corporation.

1.	A Journey must begin with a single step.
2.	An unexpected event will bring you riches
3.	Every exit is an entrance to new experiences.
4.	Your ability to juggle many tasks will take you far.
5.	Your skills will accomplish what the force of many cannot, so share.
6.	Adverse/Catastrophic situations can create either failure or bring the very best out of Entrepreneurs!
7.	Wrong doing will come full circle at some point in life
8.	To successfully achieve, to lose by others & to achieve greater.
9.	To create a circle of trust, avoid all people that lends a flag
10.	Observation of others gradually will reflect good or bad
11.	Success is so hard to achieve & so hard to maintain that can be lost in a second . . . who will take the risk
12.	Always stride towards success & rule out failure
13.	People bring adversity . . . look closely at their angle of persuasion.

14.	Reach for God's vision . . . your vision will be in alignment
15.	Perception for Progress
16.	Perception of Excellence!
17.	Positioning for Success!
18.	Persistence for Positioning!
19.	Persistent Persuasion to Maximum Positioning!
20.	Pursuit
21.	Pursuit of Excellence!
22.	The Power of Persuasion!
23.	The Power of Pursuit!
24.	The Power of Strategic Pursuit!
25.	The Power of Strategic Excellence through TEAMING!
26.	Pinnacle
27.	Pinnacle of Power within Self!
28.	Pinnacle of Power through Faith!
29.	Process of Success by TEAMING!
30.	Wisdom
31.	The Achievement of Wisdom brings Success!
32.	Business by Biblical Strategic Support to Success
33.	Read up, show up, listen up . . . follow through!
34.	Research and Due Diligence provides an extraordinary means to business success!
35.	False illusion
36.	False illusions can create false success!
37.	False illusions can be derived by untrusted resources or people!
38.	Don't start your business by selling your soul
39.	Failure: Taking a leap of Contract pursuit prior to proper preparation.
40.	Form a Business Structure or stand with no support.
41.	Art of Distraction
42.	Teaming Imagination
43.	Illusions of Success
44.	Illusions of Failure
45.	The Concept to Conclusion through Complexity

46.	What you place in your business reaps the Results
47.	What you place in your business reaps the Results of Failure or Success!
48.	Cultivate to Motivate Relationships
49.	Complexity to Simplicity to Success
50.	Mentorship works with the correct Mentors, don't get caught up in the glitter of the exterior
51.	Define your Mentorship by what builds you to success.
52.	You know you have value when people of the greatest attach to you!
53.	Partnering with the best by no request reveals greatness!
54.	Always secure your internal and external source of your business
55.	Strength and Endurance
56.	Strive to achieve Inner and Outer Success!
57.	Strategic Teaming to Tactical Success
58.	Breaking the Barriers in Business
59.	Having a Testimony opens your eyes to all aspects of protection!
60.	The Journey of Entrepreneurship
61.	Overcoming Adversity . . . . don't let anyone or anything stop your road to success
62.	Competitive Intelligence
63.	Give more to receive right
64.	Stay strong to strive for success
65.	To reach for ultimate success, push through all obstacles & adversity
66.	To go forward, stay in constant movement
67.	To go forward, don't let people take you backwards no matter what!
68.	To go forward, gain foresight on business intelligence!
69.	Your skills will accomplish what the force of many can not achieve!
70.	To achieve success, form Teaming.
71.	Define your ultimate purpose in business!

72.	Do your homework, or the results will be a failed test!
73.	Life is not what it always seem. Make it better every day, week, month & year
74.	Get to the root/core of any problem to bring resolution or it will get the best of you later.
75.	If you only touch the surface of the problem—that will be the extent/end of the solution.
76.	Solve for the deepest depth for resolution.
77.	Entrepreneurs have great intuition—follow it—don't second guess yourself!
78.	Don't settle for satisfaction, exceed expectations
79.	The Cost of Success!
80.	Don't let the cost of success overpower the weight of your Success!
81.	If the people attempt to steal your ideas, then you are headed in the right direction!
82.	If the best of people/organizations try to steal your ideas, then you have created the correct ideas of all times!
83.	Avoid the false misrepresentation of friendship & business relationship. Look further than the surface!
84.	Fully know your potential Teaming or Business Partner's ambition, because it could be the defilement to your business.
85.	False or incorrect knowledge can carry you down a road to disruption. Fact Check!
86.	The System—You have to fight all battles/wars . . . fight it strategically!
87.	To obtain more knowledge, surround yourself with smarter people
88.	To avoid losing business knowledge, don't partner with untrusted resources!
89.	To obtain loyal friends, surround yourself with people of high integrity!
90.	To bring success forward, you have to define the sources of failure!
91.	No need to worry! You will always have everything that you need by your belief of Faith!

92.	Prepare Prior to the Pursuit of Anything!
93.	Structure to Strategic System to Success!
94.	Prior Planning Prevents Poor Performance
95.	Faith First and everything follows!
96.	God puts people in our lives for a reason and a season!
97.	It may not be today, but another tomorrow is coming!
98.	It may not be today, tomorrow or soon, but stay determined and the day of success will arrive in the near future!
99.	An "SDVOSB" certification is a license to hunt, not a right to a contract.
100.	An "8A Certification" is a license to hunt, not a right to a contract!
101.	An "SDVOSB" certification is an earned right by Veterans and should be respected!
102.	Be "Significant" not successful because "Success" comes with great "Significance".
103.	Stand for God or fail for everything else!
104.	Repeat (Rehearse) problems, you emerge the worst!
105.	Business problems normally derive from lack of due diligence or the envy of others!
106.	Good & Bad, be thankful for God has taught you! Repeat Good and dismiss bad!
107.	Do not fear people . . . . don't worry about what they think!
108.	There will be Haters when you proceed to the next level of success, discover them quickly!
109.	There will be Doubters! Don't agree with them! Disregard them!
110.	The untold success story!
111.	Don't let mediocrity break you down on getting to the next level.
112.	Some people want to technically defeat you, don't waste time fighting them, keep reaching for your precise targeted goals.
113.	People that you know who approaches you with bad intentions should be defined with limitations in your business positioning!
114.	Brick versus Stone: Be like a stone, not a brick. Brick is a mix & shaped and STONE is made by God, natural & has its own unique shape, don't be like others, be yourself, like a stone!

115.	Credibility brings continuous continuity of resources.
116.	Faith conquers Failure and Structure creates Success!
117.	Set your own ceiling of success, don't let society set your trend.
118.	To gain a lot, to lose it all, to achieve success (greater).
119.	Observation is the vision to success and the ability to prevent problems.
120.	Wrongly intended people, provides a "Point of Interruption (POI)".
121.	You can fail many times, but it takes one time to get up again!
122.	You can fail many times, but it takes only one time to reach success!
123.	No matter how difficult, push through!
124.	No matter how difficult things may seem, the "Achievement of Success" brings much greater satisfaction!
125.	Success is the achievement of overcoming failure.
126.	Success is the result of not accepting failure.
127.	People who do you wrong, let them go and move forward.
128.	People who do you wrong will receive their day of failure, don't waste your efforts on revenge!
129.	People who discourage you shouldn't be allowed to take up your time. Send them the other direction of your business!
130.	Don't get "vision drift", stay focused on your success!
131.	When times are very difficult, never let people see it on the exterior of your expression.
132.	Keep building step-by-step, you will see your advancement of growth.
133.	Accomplish every step by detail and see the layers of success grow.
134.	Start with great detail and finish with greater detail!
135.	Accommodate support and eliminate adversity.
136.	Seek credibility, gain unlimited resources.
137.	Learn from complexity, maintain simplicity
138.	One's testimony of adversity is unlimited knowledge for many!!!
139.	One's testimony of struggles brings educational resources for the mass.

140.	One's testimony of failure measures the will to be successful.
141.	One's testimony of obstacles educates the many of innovativeness to win.
142.	One's testimony of difficulty advances the ability of expertise.
143.	Determination provides motivation!
144.	Determination creates the path to Success!
145.	Entrepreneurship can cost you a phenomenal amount of stress for success.
146.	Entrepreneurship can be very rewarding, but can bring heavy burdens that some can't endure.
147.	Entrepreneurship will test your faith.
148.	All business responsibility lies in the hands of the Entrepreneur!
149.	An Entrepreneur must accept all consequences, good or bad!
150.	All business transformation must be strategic and pre-planned.
151.	Proper Planning presents strategic pathways towards success!
152.	As an Entrepreneur, never assume that information given is correct . . . . . check the facts!
153.	Observation prior to Pursuit!
154.	To be successful you have to break all barriers to business that stands in your way.
155.	Maintain direct observation at all times, but search out indirect observation greater!
156.	Learn from others' mistakes; then generate results.
157.	Stick to your faith no matter what the extreme outcome may bring.
158.	Once you accomplish success, no one can take it from you.
159.	What is your level of success?
160.	Everyone strives for success, many fail not pursuing it!
161.	Success by Teaming!
162.	Teaming by Credibility!
163.	Give respect to get respect.
164.	Don't make a business decision based on someone else's persuasion.
165.	Observe "Big Talkers", they will provide unrealistic views in a short amount of time!

166.	"Big Talkers" will sooner than later reveal their weaknesses or lack of knowledge the more they talk! Listen closer!
167.	Interview everyone three times minimum prior to hiring them.
168.	If you see a problem in someone personal character, most likely it will reflect in their business life.
169.	High dollar figures in contracts & profits should drive your motivation to do business, but not the ability to overlook others.
170.	An Entrepreneur has to surround him or herself with motivated surroundings.
171.	An Entrepreneur should align themselves with positive people and not engage with negative people.
172.	Stick to your plan of action for your business and don't let others take you on another trip.
173.	You should only do business with people that have the same or better integrity than you.
174.	Credibility brings Consistent Continuity to Committed Collaboration to Success.
175.	Don't be fooled by the persuasion of others' business class.
176.	Success by God's Design
177.	Faith will defeat failure . . . all of the time!
178.	Without Faith, you set yourself up for Failure
179.	Observe, analyze and execute!
180.	Prestigious awards and notifications happen to those who do absolute right!
181.	The measure of the success is when you receive prestigious notifications from God
182.	The measure of success is when you receive prestigious notifications to be in charge of the United States Presidential Inauguration—Commander-in-Chief Presidential Ball!
183.	Teaming relationships brings a vast amounts of resources!
184.	A Breakthrough is an Art of Breaking Barriers of any kind
185.	Find a way to get "Through" anything or be blocked by everything
186.	Every exit is an entrance to new experiences
187.	No need to worry! You will always have everything that you need if you stick to your faith

188.	Your ability to juggle many tasks will take you far
189.	Your great sense of creativity will inspire others
190.	A great leader attracts many followers
191.	To succeed, you must defeat all failures
192.	To succeed, you must eliminate sources of failure
193.	To succeed, you must overcome great adversity
194.	To succeed, you must generate a strong structure
195.	The presence of power is to achieve credibility
196.	The presence of credibility is to obtain Teaming as your primary means of business transformation!
197.	To gain credibility is to achieve great relationships
198.	To achieve great relationships lends great credibility
199.	Always aim high on your goals, you will never fall to average
200.	Always protect your business interest
201.	Protect your business first before launching it!
202.	As an Entrepreneur, add double protection for yourself
203.	As an Entrepreneur, limit your access to the unknown
204.	Always be thorough in your pursuit of business
205.	Be swift in positioning, but thorough in decision making
206.	Avoid hearing and listen to bad reasoning!
207.	Ambition is the incentive that makes purpose great and achievement greater
208.	Hope is the most precious treasure to a person
209.	You are about to embark on a delightful journey
210.	Be prepared to accept a wondrous opportunity in the days ahead
211.	You can't do everything, but don't let that be an excuse to do nothing
212.	Don't blind yourself from success by the persuasion of others, avoid false illusions!
213.	You can't help all, help the many!
214.	Don't think you can do it by yourself, you will need help from others; this is a way to success!
215.	Business is not a one track system, it is a multi-system of systems interlinking with other systems. Don't get derailed!

216.	You can fail many times; it takes the one time to get up again to succeed. Don't stay down after 100 times, 101 may be the answer to success!
217.	Ambition is the incentive that makes purpose great and achievement greater
218.	Come unprepared and leave without a second chance
219.	Come unprepared and failure will be inevitable
220.	Come prepared and you will be readily for success
221.	You can fail many times; it takes the one time to get up again.
222.	An exciting opportunity lies ahead of you
223.	Failure is the demise of success! Conquer failure strategically and completely!
224.	Never compare yourself to what others can do, but to the best you can do.
225.	Your ambitious nature will help you make a name for yourself
226.	Your greatest efforts will produce the greatness of your business brand!
227.	Live each day as though it were your last, but plan for the future
228.	Set your own destiny!
229.	Set your own destiny and eliminate the fears that follow!
230.	Your faith will carry you through any circumstance
231.	Stand-fast through any set of adversities!
232.	Success is the achievement of overcoming failure
233.	Success is the result of not accepting failure
234.	Success is the ability to accomplish what you measure as a win in your journey in life—then you achieve success
235.	What I have in control of me is what God has given us and what we don't have control of is not given by God.
236.	By God, he will never give you more than you can handle or it is not by God!
237.	Always generate positive thinking through the hardest times!
238.	To achieve success, form teaming
239.	To reach for ultimate success, push through all obstacles
240.	To go forward, stay in constant movement

241.	Stay strong to strive for success
242.	Give more to receive right
243.	Your actions will always spark a reaction that hopefully creates a great interaction to others!
244.	Success is so hard to achieve, so hard to maintain, can be lost in a blink of an eye . . . . will you take the risk and responsibility!
245.	Aim high and push higher!
246.	Success won't happen continuously long-term until you overcome the adversity
247.	Don't hold grudges so that you can receive God's glory
248.	When you are in God's favor, nothing can stop your road to success!
249.	Fight all odds and winning success will come the next day!
250.	You create your own stage and your audience is waiting!
251.	You will soon witness success, but don't wait on it, pursue it strategically!
252.	Use your abilities at this time to stay focused on your goal. You will succeed.
253.	The best revenge is massive success!
254.	Veterans seek out Success!
255.	Veterans take on challenges head on strategically to achieve Success!
256.	Veterans, accepts nothing less than Success!
257.	Know the Politics that surround your business!
258.	Know the limitations or restrictions of the politics that could impact your business!
259.	Don't get caught up on a side of politics, but the politics that support your efforts towards success!
260.	Today an idea, Tomorrow a Dream fulfilled!
261.	People try to tear me down, but I keep getting back up to achieve great success!
262.	Having support from the largest company in the world definitely confirms success and the greatest value to others!
263.	All dreams come true if we have the courage to pursue them!

264.	Why are you trying so hard to fit in when you were born to stand out!
265.	Entrepreneurs always stand out in a crowd!
266.	The happiest people don't necessarily have the best of everything but they make the most of everything!
267.	As an Entrepreneur, you should know that you are destined for greatest, don't accept anything less!
268.	As a Small Business Owner always strive for greatest within and success will flourish externally!
269.	As a Small Business Owner striving for good will make you better in business!
270.	What lies behind and before us are small measures of what lies within us!
271.	Don't expect others to do what you are not will to do!
272.	Surround yourself with only those who will help you elevate to a higher level of success!
273.	Entrepreneurial strength is derived by the measurement of overcoming all obstacles, adversity and struggles!
274.	Don't expect entrepreneurship to be easy, expect your abilities within entrepreneurship to be greater!
275.	You'll be surprised to know how far you can go from the point where you thought you needed to be unless you always strive longer than you need to go!
276.	Life is not about waiting for the storm to pass, it is about preparing to overcome the conditions of the storm before it hits you!
277.	Create your source of evolvement so that you surpass the limitations of expectations!
278.	To serve others you need to have a heart of transparency for good!
279.	Success is not what happens to you, but how you respond to accomplish what comes your way!
280.	Build yourself with trusted resources and the integrity bond will secure your business venture against the odds and opposition!

281.	If you do not put out 100% efforts in your entrepreneurial journey, how can you expect others to do good for you!
282.	If you are not in the proper business perspective, then move your placement to a better aligned perspective!
283.	Those that talk down to you are just trying to walk tall by making you feel small. Rise above it!
284.	The most rewarding goals in life you meet are often the ones that look like they were impossible to accomplish!
285.	When you stand for good, who you are speaks so loudly and clear; there is really no reason for you to shout your words; speak softly and your actions will be loud!
286.	When you should fail at something it is not whether you have failed, but what you learned from it and overcome that failure immediately for success!
287.	An unbeatable person is one that never gives up!
288.	Before you can win you have to accept that there will be no lost!
289.	When you are tired, reach hard times, struggles and adversities come your way, remember to lean towards your faith and hope to get you to the glory!
290.	What matters most in business is your ability to reach far beyond the scope of average!
291.	When you have the will to succeed fully no matter the adversity, then nothing can stop you but yourself!
292.	Opposition should be an additional fuel to drive you closer to success!
293.	Opposition by others should define your ability to drive much harder!
294.	Victory is always possible for the person who refuses to stop battling!
295.	You never lose until you quit trying to accomplish success!
296.	Ask and you shall receive, but don't get disappointment after the 100th try. Keep trying!
297.	It's not the load that breaks you down, it's the way you carry the load!

298.	Danger for most of us lies not in setting our aim towards the sky and falling to the bottom; but in setting our aim too low near the bottom & achieving our low mark!
299.	Success is something you attract by the entrepreneur you become!
300.	People that are too weak to follow their own dreams will always find a way to discourage their dreams!
301.	Do the hard task first. The easier task will take care of themselves by much smaller efforts!
302.	Talent is God given. Be humble. Fame is man-made. Be grateful!
303.	For every minute you are filled with frustration you lose sixty seconds of happiness and clarity to solve a problem!
304.	Goals are the fuel in a fine tuned engine of achievement!
305.	A friend is someone who is always there for you when he or she would rather be anywhere else!
306.	No person was ever honored for what he received. Honor has been the reward for what he or she earned!
307.	Take the first step in faith. You don't have to see the entire stairway, just take the first step of faith to get to your success!
308.	The secret of happiness is to count your blessings while others are plotting against you and casting envy against you, but you overcome all that they attempt to do!
309.	The greatest glory in living lies not in falling, but in rising on every occasion you failed!
310.	Remember happiness doesn't depend upon who you are, where you came from or what you have; it depends solely on what you accomplish that satisfies your level of success!
311.	In the most strategic alignment, at the right time, everything will be extraordinary!
312.	Go after your dreams diligently! Live the life you've imagined by the source of your dreams reached!
313.	You can't climb the ladder of success in the attire of complete failure!
314.	To be successful, you must decide precisely what you want to accomplish; then strategically figure out how to pay the price to get it!

315.	If you have never made a mistake then it means you have never tried something new or you were not willing to take the risk to achieve success!
316.	Great minds strategically develop ideas; average minds seek out ideas similar to others; and small minds borrow or steal ideas from others!
317.	People only do their best at things that are easily achieved, but accomplish success by the extreme measures of risk!
318.	You can easily judge the character of a man or woman by how he or she treats those who can do nothing for them in the pursuit of entrepreneurship!
319.	There are no mistakes made in life that are not driven by others, so learn from the mistakes so that you can defend against the more coming mistakes!
320.	Wise men or women are not always silent, but they know when to be silent or speak their words!
321.	Million dollar ideas are a dime a dozen. The ability and determination to see them through is what's most valuable!
322.	If your strength is small and limited, don't carry heavy burdens. If your words are worthless, don't provide advice to others!
323.	Winning as a team provides the greatest support. It's great to share success because failure normally comes as one!
324.	Minds are like parachutes—they are of no value until they are in continuous function!
325.	All that we are is a result of what we have thought and what we accomplish in our lives!
326.	You can't let other people tell you who you are. You have to decide that for yourself or you will be undefined!
327.	Be slow to fall into friendship; because extended time develops the true friendship!
328.	A person can succeed at almost anything for which they decide not to give up to any such adversity!
329.	Do what you can at all times, with what you have, but always strive for more at all times during your entire entrepreneurial journey!

330.	If you win by dishonorable measures, that will be no real victory!
331.	What God intended for you extends much greater than you ever could imagine in the world of entrepreneurship!
332.	If you accept the expectations presented by others, especially the negative ones, then you will never reach your outcome of success!
333.	Before you can win, you have to become of worthy character!
334.	Our deepest fear is not that we are inadequate. Our deepest fear is that we are powerful beyond measure of achieving success no matter the adversity!
335.	I can accept failure. I can fail many times. Everyone fails at something. But I can't accept not trying to overcome failure so I will always strive for success!
336.	The difference between the impossible and the possible lies in a man or woman's self-determination!
337.	No act of kindness, no matter how small, is ever misunderstood by people of great values!
338.	In life you are either a passenger or a pilot, it's your choice. Which journey will you choose!
339.	Hard life lessons in business often come unexpected in the form of adversity, roadblocks, struggles or obstacles. Will you let it break you or build you!
340.	The worth of a book is to be measured by the effort it took to develop it with a great purpose!
341.	You can't build a reputation on what you're going to do, but only as to what you have done in the form of an accomplishment!
342.	You'll be surprised to know how far you can go only if you take the risk to reach success!
343.	When anyone tells me I can't do something, it motivates me to get closer to achieving my success. I hear them, but I do not listen to them!
344.	People of accomplishment rarely sat back to receive it, they sat out to get it at no matter the cost of adversity!

345.	Adversity causes some men or women to breakdown, and others to break records!
346.	You have to believe in yourself when no one else does because this will be the key to reaching your success through the most adverse conditions!
347.	Breakthrough any adversity, barriers, obstacles, struggles to achieve success by the measures precise and strategic operational perseverance!

Appendix E

Note Pages

NOTES

NOTES

NOTES

NOTES